Community Organizing:

A Brief Introduction

By Mike Miller

Euclid Avenue Press
2329 E. Euclid, Milwaukee, WI, 53207

Published by:
Euclid Avenue Press

© Mike Miller, 2012

Body text is Times New Roman; headings are Franklin Gothic Heavy.

Cover photo from Flickr under Creative Commons Commercial license.

ISBN: 978-0615623214

Table of Contents

Introduction

"Community organizing" applies democratic ideals and practices to specific contexts. These include neighborhoods, schools, religious congregations, civic associations, union locals and other organizations that want to fully engage people in participation in public life. Its contemporary origins are in the work of Saul Alinsky whose organizing work in the late 1930s led to the development of what is now called "the Alinsky tradition."

Alinsky's approach has since been revised, modified, expanded, and elaborated to meet new circumstances, with new practices to address emerging problems. The first chapter of this book introduces one strand of community organizing that grew from the work of the Industrial Areas Foundation (IAF), headed by Alinsky until his death in 1972. This strand is variously called "institution-based" or "faith-based" community organizing. It focuses on religious congregations[1] as the principal building blocks of "people power."

This approach to community organizing draws upon the moral, and social and economic justice, teachings of the world's great religions. It engages deeply with the life of religious congregations, using action in the world on behalf of justice as a tool to renew and revitalize them. It carefully focuses on leadership development and institutional growth. Through collective action, it holds dominant political and economic institutions accountable to the common good.

Other approaches to community organizing exist as well. They have also drawn upon, modified, elaborated, and expanded on work done by Alinsky and his early associates. While brief reference to these other approaches is made in this book, a more detailed description is beyond its scope.

The second chapter of the book provides an introduction to practical political theory. It addresses the concrete experiences of people seeking to solve problems that affect the quality of their lives—problems of employment or underemployment, economic development, schools and education,

---

[1] I use "congregation" generically to refer to Catholic, Mainline Protestant, Evangelical, Pentecostal, Holiness, Non-Denominational, Jewish, Muslim and Buddhist gatherings of the faithful. There are more than fifty different denominations and faith traditions participating in the more than 100 of these organizations that now exist in almost every part of the U.S. and increasingly elsewhere in the world.

child care, housing, health care, public services, neighborhood revitalization, destruction or degradation of the environment, predatory lending and others. The theory chapter provides a framework for understanding Alinsky-tradition community organizing of whatever strand.

Finally, the third chapter of this book focuses on conflict tactics. Alinsky was often thought of simply as a tactician, becoming widely known because of his imaginative use of conflict. But Alinsky was not simply a tactician. He *used* conflict tactics as a tool to overcome feelings of powerlessness and to engage marginalized, exploited, and otherwise excluded people in democratic civic life. With these tactics, leaders in his organizations brought power structure decision makers to the negotiating table and achieved many important social changes. Alinsky's ideals were those of the democratic tradition which, at their core, say that the people are competent to, and should, rule.

Community Organizing

Power and Organizing

"Power": the ability to act effectively in the world.

Power can be used for good or evil. Tyrannical, unaccountable power is abusive. Another kind of power emerges when large numbers of people act together to pursue democratic ideals and solve social problems. This kind of "people power" is exercised through large, participatory organizations that don't spring spontaneously into being. This book explores one approach to building people power that is based for the most part in religious congregations—churches, mosques, temples and synagogues. The organizations that these religious bodies together form are the result of activities of thousands of people, the inspiration and perspiration of hundreds of local leaders acting through their existing "mediating institutions" and, in some cases, through newly created organizational forms. They are assisted in this by the presence of a highly-skilled professional organizer. These broadly-based community organizations now number about 200 nationwide; the professional organizers who build them number between two and five hundred. Just seventy years ago, the field didn't exist.

Stripped to the essentials, the job of the community organizer is to help the people build a powerful organization rooted in the values of the democratic tradition and the moral, social, and economic justice teachings of the world's great religious traditions.

The Professional Organizer, Her Network, and the Beginning of an Organizing Process

Current major community organizing efforts all have professional organizing staff who assist local leadership in creating, maintaining, and expanding powerful organizations. The first organizer in one of these organizations is typically an outsider. Because the people inside the community have histories of rivalry, any initiative taken by a local person or group is likely to leave out some people and groups, heightening conflict. If there was a local person who could have developed such an organization, it is likely she would have done it. An organizer, specifically identified with none, can work for all. Further, in historically powerless, or relatively powerless communities there is little experience with large, complex, organizations that confront institutional power.

The story of "broadly-based community organizing" can best be told through the histories of representative individuals and their neighborhoods, cities or metropolitan areas. Here, I draw upon the true history of one organizing effort, with added material from other true stories, to form a composite. I have called the city "American City," and the organizer "Jeanne Steuben."

A local group of religious leaders contacted a national organizing network to introduce broadly-based community organizing in American City. The network that Jeanne Steuben belonged to conducted workshops and invited local leaders to attend longer national sessions. The initial two founding clergymen, Rev. Ben Walker and Fr. John Sullivan, attended a longer workshop in another city where there was already a "congregation-based community organization." They were the "internal organizers" who initially moved the project forward in American City. In the three years before Jeanne Steuben arrived, almost fifty people participated in the longer network-sponsored workshops, and over two hundred in local, shorter, ones.

Before Steuben arrived in American City, then, a good deal of organizing had actually taken place, resulting in the formation of a formal "Sponsor Committee"—the group that enables the community organization to be born. It raises funds, hires an organizer and network and legitimizes—or "credentials" as organizers call it—the organizing effort. Typically, it does not engage in action on issues. Walker and Sullivan pulled together the American City Sponsor Committee comprised of local denominational leaders, and respected pastors and lay leaders over a three-year period. They talked individually with other pastors and raised small amounts of local denominational "seed money" for introductory workshops. Their patient work ultimately gave birth to the full Sponsor Committee. This larger group raised the initial budget to hire the organizer and her network from congregation, denomination and foundation sources.

The formation of the Sponsor Committee took three quiet years because the national organizing network and the local organizing project initiators wanted breadth of involvement "on the ground floor" before the effort was made public or took action on issues. They knew that something which surfaced in the news media would look well established. People coming in after reading a news story often feel they are joining someone else's creation and tend to be more passive members. The goal of the project's initiators was to have a broadly-based group of people "owning" the effort from its inception. Further, while the Sponsor Committee had general agreement on problems to be addressed by an independent community organization, they also understood that the particular issues would emerge from the people themselves.

In the network workshops participants learned about community organizing and its relationships to the American democratic tradition, to the teachings of their own religious faith, and to the specific problems facing them, their members, their neighbors and their congregations. More than anything else, they learned, at least in the abstract, that building an organization was more important than any particular issue. In fact, they came to realize that this organization-building was the key to an effective struggle for justice, whatever the issue might be. Sponsor Committee members also discovered that in the Catholic Church and Mainline Protestant denominations there was a history of support for this kind of organizing. Policy statements, theological study materials, and financial support were all available from national church-related agencies.

The national workshops, sponsored by the various organizing networks, have another purpose as well. The workshops particularly challenge religious leaders to deal with their ambivalence about, and fear of using, power—a precondition to effective action in behalf of justice in the world. Pastors also recognize that they will have to develop more accountable mechanisms within their own congregations. For those who were solo spokespersons for "their people," a new relationship will have to be developed—both with the "downtown" decision-makers they may have encountered in the past, and with their own members.

Once in American City to begin full-time work, Jeanne Steuben's first task was to have individual meetings with the leaders on the Sponsor Committee and identify additional potential participants. Individual one-to-one meetings are the heart of building a community organization. When she visited clergy of churches or other congregations not on the Sponsor Committee, Jeanne was introduced by those who were. Rather than arriving as a total stranger, she was "credentialed" by respected people. And within the congregations that had representatives on the Sponsor Committee were leaders who had already attended lengthy workshops on community organizing who had been identified by the pastor and/or other core leaders of the congregations. She wanted to meet people who were respected by others; through them she would do her organizing work. Each of them, respected by a circle of perhaps ten-to-twenty people within the congregation and, perhaps, by neighbors or co-workers, are the operational leaders in the effort to build a local organization. Jeanne and the already committed leaders sought to draw into this "organizing drive" others they knew and others with whom they began to develop relationships. For example, within Fr. Sullivan's parish there were different age, racial/ethnic (mostly Irish and Hispanic), gender and interest groups. Jeanne also made sure she met with representative leaders from the different formal and informal sub-groupings in the congregations.

The organizer's tools are listening, challenging, thinking through, and training. Through a careful listening process the organizer learns the hopes, pains, dreams and frustrations of local leaders. Organizers use what they hear to challenge leaders to act. It is this mix of listening and challenging that gives the organizer her reputation as an "outside agitator." At her best, that is precisely what she is.

Having heard the pains and frustrations, as well as the hopes and dreams of local leaders, Jeanne Steuben was in a position to challenge people to act and challenge rationales for inaction. When appeals to vision and values, on the one hand, and individual and institutional concerns or interests, on the other, failed to move them, she would move on, trying to leave the door open for future conversations. Her "organizing plan" anticipated visits to many more institutional leaders than would actually seek to bring their congregations into the community organization as a member. For each one who was willing to engage in the exploration of organizing there were multiple visits to deepen the relationship and broaden the understanding of organizing.

In the best organizing practice, the local leaders on the Sponsor Committee combine access to funds and strong relationships in the constituencies targeted for the organizing project. This formal procedure emerged out of the early pioneering work in this field by Saul Alinsky (1909-1972), whose Industrial Areas Foundation now carries on his work. Similarly, though not with as elaborate a form, the Student Nonviolent Coordinating Committee, when it began voter registration work in Mississippi in the early 1960s, was legitimized by a network of local black leaders, working in chapters of the NAACP and local voters' leagues. These leaders invited the SNCC workers into their communities to help them break the barrier to voting rights and the state's wall of institutionalized segregation.

Leaders

Organizers have a core meaning for "leader." As Saul Alinsky put it, "when you boil it all down, a leader is someone with a following." In all places where there are regularized human relationships, there are also local leaders. Jeanne Steuben targeted the Rev. Walker and Fr. Sullivan, their counterparts, and lay leaders within each of the participating congregations for individual meetings. She had hundreds of such meetings in her effort to develop the organization. The followings of such leaders may be relatively small, but when added together they amount to a powerful base for action. And, in most communities, there are leaders of the leaders.

In Fr. Sullivan's parish, with 2,000 families on the rolls, there were many leaders—though Fr. Sullivan hadn't been thinking of them in that way. In fact, he saw many as obstacles rather than potential assets. He had been giving anti-racism homilies, and wondered why he'd gotten such a negative re-action. "You know, Father," Jeanne said bluntly, "you want people to be where you think they ought to be, but you have to start where they are." "But Jeanne," he said, "aren't you against racism?" "Of course," she replied, "but I want to find out how to move other people to be against it as well, and you've told me yourself that hitting them over the head with the immorality of it isn't moving them." Fr. Sullivan remembers that conversation as one of his "ah-hah" moments in organizing.

Institutional leaders, like the clergy and lay leaders on the Sponsor Committee, worry about the pressures taking a toll on the lives of the people in their communities. Most depressing are a pervasive sense of hopelessness, and the absence of any effective way to work to combat the pressures. These are distinct from another set of pressures—those on the congregations as organizations. Leaders have interests in solving the problems of "their people," and in maintaining and building their institutions. Institutionally-based community organizing addresses both. Indeed, it is not until an organizer can persuade a pastor that organizing addresses both that most pastors will invest themselves. Otherwise, the idea of another major "new program" would be discouraging. It is because the process of organizing offers a way to build a deeper community than one built on endless programs that many pastors decide to become involved.

Summing up what she heard from her hundreds of visits, Jeanne made the following analysis of the problems of the institutions and their leaders targeted for her American City organizing work:

Pastors, civic, and other leaders often experienced a substantial gap between what they hoped to accomplish and what they did every day in their organizations. Many were frustrated because their day-to-day work often had little to do with the ideals that led them to their leadership positions in the first place. The problems of maintaining an organization felt all-consuming, leaving little time for reflection, for envisioning a better future, or for long-range planning.

These leaders were plagued by scarcities: not enough leaders to share the burdens (and joys) of leadership; not enough members, volunteers or workers to keep the programs of the organization alive; not enough money and time. The absence of one was related to absences of others. The scarcity led to the syndrome of the same old people getting stretched thinner and thinner, all the while complaining about those who weren't participating. As a result, people were on the edge of burnout. Others had already dropped out. Cynicism was increasing. "Apathy" was a very popular word.

Many leaders were embroiled in seemingly unmanageable internal conflicts. Rivalries among leaders went beyond healthy competition. In some of the churches, like Fr. Sullivan's, there were ethnic, age, gender and other group conflicts. Groups and individuals struggled over resources, with little sense that, whatever the disagreements, "we're in this together" because we share a faith that calls us to be the leaven in the world.

Local leaders felt imposed on by higher-level decision-making bodies ("They don't listen to the people in the trenches.") The higher-level leaders and program staff felt unappreciated for the work they were doing and leadership they were trying to provide ("They're so parochial down there," or, "You can never get them to listen to a new idea.")

Some of the leaders had been engaged in issues, joining "coalitions" for or against a cause important to them, often reacting to crises resulting from decisions made without them or their people at the decision-making table. They felt they were always reacting to someone else's agenda. At best, they were able to stop some of the worst things from happening. More often, after a protracted battle, with diminishing participation over time on the part of those adversely affected, they had lost, sometimes after a big demonstration that had no follow-up behind it.

Expecting the impossible from themselves, institutional leaders tended to engage in self-blame for the problems. They doubted their own worth and feared that those they were supposed to lead didn't think they were right for the job. At the same time, they often lacked the training and skills needed to address the problems. They also lacked productive contexts for reflection, action and study. They craved engagements that could transform problems into opportunities for constructive action, connect deeply-held values with daily life, and build and deepen a sense of community in their organizations and neighborhoods.

Many of the leaders felt under siege. Rarely did they get to reflect on their hopes and dreams, or share them with one another, or with the people for whom they provide leadership. The sense of isolation was widespread. Many felt they had no one to talk with about their deepest concerns. They seemed alone in their struggles, finding little or no support within their congregations or in their broader community. From a consumer-driven perspective, they saw themselves as inadequate providers for those who were their "markets." Simultaneously, and contradictorily, they had deep doubts about the "success" of organizations that appear to be built on media-hype and show.

How could they be leaders for their people, they asked themselves, when their own spirits were so low? Part of the message that Jeanne Steuben brought was that a key barrier to change was their own assumption that it was *their* job to maintain and build their organizations, rather than increasingly involving *others* in maintaining and building community and organization.

Our mediating institutions, including religious congregations, are in trouble in large part because a growing number of their members are only peripherally involved in them. The key to the renewal of the spirit of the leaders is to renew the organizations by challenging members to play a qualitatively different role in them. The magic of the organizing process is to include ever increasing numbers of people in such organizations.

Mediating Institutions

Voluntary associations, like religious congregations, can be renewed by the deepening sense of mission in the world that participation in a broadly-based community organization gives them. Their capacity is strengthened by a growing ability to address specific material and spiritual problems facing their members and neighbors, by the character and quality of their communal life, and by the practical lessons of leadership training that a professional organizer and network provides. In conversation after conversation, returning to the experiences of the people with whom she was speaking, Jeanne addressed these themes. She made general principles of organizing real by relating them to each person's particular circumstances and experiences.

In the best community organizations, individuals and organizations see the organizing effort as an extension of their own interests and values—not an imposition on them. They understand that individuals and families need to be part of something larger for them to have any hope of grappling effectively with the pressures undermining their values and ability to survive. Individual voluntary associations need to become part of something larger if they want to effectively act on the values they profess, to deal with problems facing their members and neighbors, and to respond to the problems of organizational renewal many of them face. Most Americans are desperately looking for a community that is significant, that offers a sense of place and belonging which nourishes and sustains them and in which they can play significant roles. Time is still scarce, but citizenship and active membership will supersede consumership (the passive kind of sitting at the TV or computer screen and the "active" kind of strolling the mall) if voluntary associations can give effective expression to peoples' deepest values and hopes.

America's voluntary institutions are known throughout the world for their role in our democracy. They are called "mediating institutions" because they stand between the mega-institutions of government and business, on the one hand, and families and individuals on the other. Most analysts of American society agree on the importance of "civil society" and its institutions which defend people from the excesses of dominant economic and political institutions. These can be the incubators of new social and political initiatives in behalf of democratic values. At the local level, they are the places where families and individuals learn and act on values, develop skills and self-confidence, build a sense of mutual support and community, tackle local problems, sponsor clubs, and more. They often provide sources of deep meaning for their members.

Mediating institutions are the base of "civil society," the patterns of associational life that exist independent of the state and government. Furthermore, these institutions generate of what scholars now call "social capital"— the webs of relationships, trust and informal leadership that undergird democratic societies. This "social capital" characteristically emerges from congregations, athletic teams and leagues, senior and youth clubs, parent organizations, unions, small business, homeowner and tenant groups—that is from voluntary membership organizations.

The most deeply rooted of these institutions in most communities are local congregations.

The Centrality of Religious Congregations

This section introduces some of the theoretical ideas underling the American City organizing approach. It uses material from three of the major organizing networks, and identifies others. This material provides a context for the American City story.

"Organizing for Family and Congregation" is the seminal paper on congregation-based community organizing, prepared by the Industrial Areas Foundation (IAF) under the direction of its Executive Director, Ed Chambers. It is both an elaboration of Alinsky's earlier involvement with the religious community. Here are portions of that document.

> Our country is in…crisis…. The intermediate voluntary institutions— including churches—are ineffectual in a power relationship with the powerful. As a result, the middle is collapsing, confused. The economic and political middle of this country is being sucked dry by a vacuum—a vacuum of power and values. Into that vacuum have moved the huge corporations, mass media and "benevolent" government…. If families and churches which are clear about their Judeo-Christian value base do not develop the capacity to negotiate institutionally, the masses of American families will continue to feel a decreasing sense of integration, centeredness and confidence in their own relationship to other institutions. Families and churches, as instruments of nurture, clarity and protection for their members, will continue to lose their capacity to be effective.
>
> …
>
> The modern American family has become a money machine. Month after

month it must meet the food bills, mortgage or rent, car and other transportation costs, insurance premiums, non-insured health items, clothing costs, taxes, utilities and fuel, school tuition and expenses, recreation, entertainment and travel, home maintenance, appliance costs, cosmetics and drugs, and contributions to charity and to churches. Churches have similar burdens, plus staggering building maintenance costs, denominational assessments, and staff salaries to pay.

A second set of pressures comes from the immediate physical community. Almost every community is beginning to feel the accumulated corrosive effect of [crime, environmental degradation], alcohol abuse, drug abuse, pornography.... These conditions, some subtle, some obvious, combine to kill the spirit....

The third set of pressures is cultural. Television is a profoundly parochial medium with an almost universal range. The networks transmit the simplistic values of the advertisers—basically money, luxury, and sanitized sex...Television tells people how to eat, how to look, how to love, how to kill, and how to feel. It throws out powerful images of what it is to be human—images frequently destructive of healthy family values. It devours space in family homes—where a TV room is now common—and it devours time that families could use together.

The final form of cultural pressure is work—the expectation that work schedules are more important than family schedules, and the pressures that force those parents to work. In half the families with school-age children, both parents must work to fuel the family money machine, to meet the basic costs of keeping the family alive. Too often, what they work so hard for is undone by their own hard work. The child who leaves a struggling school, who walks down dangerous streets, often arrives at an empty, parentless home, or to parents so strapped by the demands of work, the tensions and frustrations of an environment seemingly out of their control, that they have no energy left for the love and care of their children.

Institutional Power

Our dollars end up in banks and savings and loans, in insurance companies, in oil companies, in utilities, and in the hands of major manufacturers, real estate developers, retailers, and organized criminals. These people speak with money. Banks, insurance companies, and organized crime provide capital for the others. They buy the second level, the politicians, lawyers, the advertisers, the media...Lawyers and other professionals provide the rationales and jargon to perpetuate the top power institutions and screen them from the public. These professionals also do a lot of negotiating with the government bureaucracies and pass back and forth between government and private jobs, especially at the upper-middle levels.

...

Decisions made by primary power institutions (banks, insurance companies, developers, financial institutions, major manufacturers, large retailers and organized crime)—institutions built upon the money of families and con-gregations—obviously have a major impact on the congregations and their families.

...

The point is not that all executives of all banks and corporations in America are bad men. Rather, the point is that profit is the bottom line val-ue of their institutions, and that "the system" is blind to the destruction of churches and families. So long as families and churches exhaust themselves with the middle men, so long as families and churches struggle with the politicians and the bureaucrats, the alignment of power will remain the same. The deterioration of family and congregational life will continue. The economic, cultural, and community pressures will increase to an intolerable point. The institutions that cause those pressures, mammoth machines lack-ing eyes, ears, and sensitivities, will continue, by instinct, to stamp society in their own images."

The IAF paper concludes:

[Building these organizations] is as complex and critical as the raising of a family, as the growth of a congregation. In isolation, families and congrega-tions have no chance. With the citizens' organization as a context and as an instrument, families and congregations can move with dignity and confi-dence into the arena of institutional power. Families and congregations can fight for their values. Families and congregations can win."

Greg Galluzzo, recently-retired Executive Director of the Gamaliel Foun-dation, an organizing network in the Alinsky tradition focused on congrega-tions, describes five models of church:

- *Charismatic/spiritual/fundamentalist churches.* These tend to believe that their work should be about saving souls. The work of justice should either be left to the Lord or is irrelevant to our times. On the other hand, and contradictorily, these churches are often supporters of a very conservative political agenda.
- *Charitable/social service/works of mercy churches.* These take satis-faction in helping the victims of injustice, but do not want to examine or address the causes of injustice. The people usually helped by such churches do not become part of the worshipping community. In some cases members of such churches would argue that any attempt to make them part of the worshipping community would be to place inappro-priate expectations on the services they provide.
- *Prophetic churches.* These speak out strongly against injustice, but do not create the means to be able to affect it. They identify issues and causes they believe to be just and publicly address them, both in word

and deed. Whether their action leads to results in the public arena is not a central criteria in the determination of what they do. They see their task as being faithful, whether effective or not.

- *Alternative community churches.* These build a wall between themselves and the surrounding society. They offer themselves as a model of how a satisfactory, Christian life could be lived. They separate themselves from the vast majority of the people. Like prophetic churches, they are unwilling to build power sufficient to engage power, to use power against power. They believe that their alternative model will, if effectively communicated to others, grow and become a substitute for the unjust systems that now prevail.

"All four types, "Galluzzo argues, "can profess a naïve innocence because they do not involve themselves in the difficult and not always unambiguous business of influencing the structures, policies and practices of public institutions (government, nonprofit, or profit)." The second and third types, Galluzzo believes, have proven to be ineffective in maintaining and strengthening congregations. The fourth type may build a strong congregation, but is incapable of wider influence because its demands for entry exclude most people.

Galluzzo then identifies a fifth type:

- *Church-based organizing.* This approach involves churches that are willing to roll up their sleeves and help rebuild community and create enough power to impact social policy. This church also knows that it must itself be strong numerically and financially to be viable and to play a role impacting change. It invests in the development of its lay people. It knows that the greatest gift it has to offer is the church itself and not charity or programs. It takes seriously the intentional building of community both within and without the congregation. It works ecumenically so that the ecclesia (membership body of the church or, in this case, all participating churches) can be manifest here on earth.

Key documents from another congregation-focused organizing network working out of the Alinsky tradition, People Improving Communities through Organizing (PICO), describe core procedures for its "faith-based" organizing work. PICO has become increasingly prominent, with national influence on issues of health care reform, immigration, and the mortgage/foreclosure crisis. Below, I quote from various PICO documents to provide the essence of their thinking, which provides a good example of the best thinking, today, around faith-based organizing:

Faith-Based Community Organizing is a method of working with faith communities to address the problems and concerns of their communities, and in turn, vitalize and strengthen the life of congregations.

...

PICO's path to building a more just world involves teaching people of faith how to build and exercise their own power to address the root causes of the problems they face. In PICO, this struggle for justice is rooted in our faith.

At the center of PICO's model of faith-based community organizing is a belief in the potential for transformation – of people, institutions, and our larger culture. This belief stems directly from PICO's rootedness in faith communities, and radiates throughout the organization, influencing the way PICO relates to public officials, to community members, and to one another.

...

PICO builds community organizations based on religious congregations, schools and community centers, which are often the only stable civic gathering places in many neighborhoods. As a result PICO federations are able to engage thousands of people and sustain long-term campaigns to bring about systematic change at all levels of government.

PICO helps congregations identify and solve local neighborhood issues before addressing broader issues at a city, state or national level. As a result PICO federations are deeply rooted in local communities.

...

PICO believes:

- ...in the potential for transformation—of people, institutions, and of our larger culture—and the power of people of faith to lead this transformation.
- ...that people should have a say in the decisions that shape their lives. We trust democracy—the original principle of the American Revolution that organized and vigilant citizens are the best defense against special interests.
- ...that ordinary people know best what their families and communities need and that their voices need to be at the center of political life. One of our basic principles is "never do for others what they can do for themselves." Ordinary people, given the proper training, motivation and support can take extraordinary steps to improve the quality of life for their communities.
- ...that when people have power they can protect the things that are important to their families and their communities, and that one way to have power is to build strong, broad-based, democratic organizations.
- ...that strong democratic organizations are rooted in the needs and resources of local communities.
- ...that government can play a vital role in improving society, but that civic leaders and organizations need to have the power to shape policy and hold public officials accountable.

- …that family is a value that motivates participation in public life and that across economic levels most American families share common concerns for good schools, affordable housing, safe neighborhoods, high quality health care, civil rights and civic participation.
- …that religion brings us together rather than divides America; that our varied faith traditions call on us to act to make our communities and our nation better places to live.
- …that the immigrant experience is a universal American story, that as we build strong communities and a strong nation, we need to insure that new Americans are welcomed and not exploited.

PICO values the racial, ethnic, religious and regional diversity that has shaped American society.

In 2011, a national group of PICO clergy issued a broad statement of vision and purpose that concludes with this:

> We pledge to teach, preach and organize to unify people of faith around reducing poverty and increasing economic and racial justice. We will challenge our elected leaders from both parties to put the needs of working families, the poor and the common good of our nation ahead of short-term political calculus and special interests. Join us in making America a land of opportunity for all people.

Other organizing networks like Direct Action Research and Training (DART) and InterValley Project (IVP) make religious congregations central to their work. Together, these networks now represent several million people engaged in action in behalf of social and economic justice and democratic participation in the United States, and they are developing a presence in Africa, Asia, Europe and Latin America. For the most part, they now engage in alliances with other community organizing groups, labor unions and others so that they can reach the critical mass of people power required for more significant impact on public and corporate policy. They constitute one of the most hopeful signs on today's political landscape.

Congregations Alone are Not Enough

Local religious institutions have always been at the center of "institutionally-based" community organizing efforts. Some summary observations can be made as to why. The earliest Alinsky organizations included all voluntary associations of a community. By the mid-1970s, however, most of these organizational forms were either atrophied (labor unions being the prime example) or effectively coopted, dependent on grants from government, foundations, corporations, or others. "Community-based nonprofit organizations" created new, and often more responsive, services, while absorbing former community leaders into program administration. Surveying this scene, some organizers in the Alinsky tradition decided that religious congregations offered the only value-based, stable organizations in many low- to moderate-income communities. They also had substantial numbers of people, and while some were on "mission status," many got their budgets from their members. The organizer formula, "organized people plus organized money = power" was met. These were the clear positives of the approach.

But this sole focus on local congregations ignored other remaining formal and informal voluntary associations. It also ignored people who were not involved in any organization.

A somewhat different approach drew upon the work of Alinsky's early associate Fred Ross (of whom Cesar Chavez said, "he's our secret weapon"), and more particularly on some of the experience of the 1960s National Welfare Rights Organization. Best exemplified by the statewide reconstituted organizations of the now defunct Association of Community Organizations for Reform Now (ACORN), this approach seeks to involve individuals directly in their organizations.

For good reason, however, this distinction between "organization based" and "individual based" community organizing is now becoming blurred. Congregation-based organizing projects now often seek the membership of other voluntary associations and institutions and initiate organizing efforts in constituencies which they cannot effectively reach through congregations, including public school parents, low-wage workers and alienated youth. For their part, direct membership organizations are looking more carefully at existing networks and organizations. They now are sometimes the initiators of, or participants in, coalitions formed to increase the power of all the participants.

Both direct membership and congregation-based approaches seek initial sponsorship from legitimizing institutions, including congregations, unions, and others. ACORN participated in coalitions to win such things as its multicity "living wage" campaigns. Similarly, the new statewide organizations that have arisen from former ACORN relationships engage in such coalitions as well. Ultimately, neither approach can afford to ignore important interests within its constituencies. When they do, the opposition will use this oversight to use "divide and conquer" tactics against organizing efforts. This argument over strategy, over the "right people" or the "right institutions" to organize, which assumes there is some simple, abstract, correct "answer" relevant to all times and all contexts, often reminds me of the medieval scholastics arguments about how many angels could dance on the head of a pin.

To fill out the picture of major Alinsky-tradition community organizing networks, The Midwest Academy, National Training and Information Center and Western Organization of Resource Councils are additional groups.

The story that follows explores one way these different approaches are often brought together by engaging congregations with the communities beyond their walls.

Institutional Renewal, Civic Action, and an Expanding Community: The Story of New Life Community Church[2]

Jeanne Steuben's visits with the lay and clergy leaders of many congregations provided the material for her analysis of the institutional problems facing the congregations as organizations. By the end of several months in American City, she knew more about the city, particularly from the point of view of its low- to middle-income people and the congregations of which they were members, than just about anyone in town. She had won the confidence of many, many people and their stories had poured out to her; she had "earned the right to meddle" because she had built relationships of trust with local leaders. It was time to move into action. One of the first action campaigns came in a church whose pastor had not been part of the Sponsor Committee, but whom she met in the course of her person-to-person, individual meetings.

New Life Community Church appeared to be dying. The handwriting was on the wall, though members were trying not to read it. Sixty-five people, median age 55, remained in the congregation, located in a near-inner-city, largely Latino, neighborhood in American City. But the new pastor, Rev. Lindner, made a commitment to try to build a loving and faithful community, one that would act on its faith and values, and to use congregation-based community organizing as the vehicle for the renewal effort. He made this decision after a number of careful conversations with American City Community Organization (ACCO) organizer Jeanne Steuben.

As a first step, Jeanne visited seven respected leaders of the congregation, referred to her by their pastor. Some held church offices; others didn't. She listened and probed—determining their vision for the church, their hopes and fears, the problems they faced in their lives, and the problems faced by the church and its neighborhood. She listened for sources of real pain, problems that were affecting the members and their families. First, there was grief over their declining church, a body that had been "home" for many of them over much of their lives. Second, crime and the fear of it, with an accompanying

---

[2] This story is drawn from an article written by Marilyn Stranske and Mike Miller.

sense of powerlessness, were common themes. Jeanne asked if they would be willing to attend a meeting to share these concerns with each other to determine what they might do together about them. The leaders agreed; they and their pastor came to the meeting.

As they gathered, they discovered the first community building lesson. By sharing their pain, they overcame a sense of isolation; it was a healing process. They then explored what community organizing would mean in their congregation and, after two such meetings, agreed to participate in a training session to learn how to visit members of the church. By the end of five weeks most of the congregation had been visited in personal meetings. At a congregation meeting attended by thirty-five, it was agreed that neighborhood crime was a major concern. Further, they decided they would start visiting neighborhood people who weren't in the church to see how they felt about neighborhood crime. Eighteen people signed up to do the visiting.

Jeanne worked with the eighteen to come up with a home-visiting plan, and trained them to do the visits. "Hi, we're your neighbors from New Life Church," visitors said, "but we haven't been very good neighbors because we haven't been talking with others who are here. We're concerned about crime in the area. We're wondering how it is for you and your family." People were eager to pour out the problems they were experiencing in the increasingly crime-ridden neighborhood. More than four hundred visits were made. Many indicated a desire to do something about crime. Six "drug houses" always came up. People were invited to be part of solving the problems, and no expectation was created that the church visitors would do it alone "for" the people of the neighborhood.

The visiting team met frequently to review their experiences. Every meeting began with a reflection led initially by the pastor, then by one of the members. During reflections, group members discussed how a passage of scripture related to tasks and problems at hand. Jeanne and the pastor assisted the leaders in preparing their reflections. Many had never before reflected in this way on Bible passages about community, justice or relationships with neighbors and their daily life as a community of faith. Each meeting provided time for a "report in" regarding their visits as well as a training and education. Participants discussed questions such as, "What did we learn?" and "What did we accomplish?"

The education began to deepen as members, joined by some neighborhood residents who were invited to become part of the group because of their positive response, initiated a research phase. They visited all agencies and officials having authority over the drug houses. More training took place, now specifically aimed at questions like, "Who has authority to do something about the drug houses?" The leaders were engaging in their first institutional power analysis: determining who decides what, who s/he answers to, and what pressures s/he might be under. (In fact, shortly after arriving in the city, Jeanne Steuben had already conducted a general power analysis that had revealed the key institutions of American City and the principal decision-makers within them. But it was important that the New Life and neighborhood leaders learned this process themselves, and apply it to their particular circumstance.) They determined that the Police Department was the appropriate authority to approach, and that the precinct captain was the person with the authority to act on the problem. Their questions then became, "How do we get the precinct captain to meet with us?" "What do we want from him?" "How do we deal with him when he comes?" "What if he won't agree to what we want?" Leadership rotation in the meetings of the group created many opportunities for individual growth, as well as allowing members to assess who they might later select as more permanent leaders.

Three New Life Church members and one neighborhood leader secured a date from the Precinct Captain for a meeting with the community at the church. As the date for the meeting came near, the visiting team reached out to everyone they had initially contacted. Contacts were invited to the public meeting; it opened with a reflection and testimony given by many of the people present. Jeanne had prepared a negotiating committee in the art of keeping a public decision-maker focused on the subject of the meeting, and preventing him from avoiding the concerns of the community. Extensive role-playing sessions were used, in which Jeanne played the precinct captain. At the meeting, the key spokesperson, a middle-aged Hispanic who had never done anything like this in her life, asked the Captain the critical questions: "Will you commit to investigate and close down the offending houses—'yes' or 'no'?" and "Will you report back to us on your progress within a month—'yes' or 'no'?" When he answered affirmatively, the spokeswoman almost fainted with relief and the crowd was jubilant. A post-meeting evaluation, open to all attendees and led by Jeanne drew lessons from the experience. Many people from the neighborhood participated. A celebratory note was struck when one of the church members said, "Now our church has a face in the neighborhood, and the face is mine."

During the evaluation, the spokespeople for the meeting described their fear in dealing with the Captain, especially as they asked sharply focused questions. This moment of confrontation was critical to the development of people taking responsibility for their community and learning to hold their officials accountable. In this process, repeated with variation in each of eleven of the congregations that decided to move into the action phase of organizing, people shifted from either internalized oppression (denying they have problems or blaming themselves for them) or victimhood (complaining about but not acting on their problems) to active responsibility to bring about change. Everyone talked about how well they had organized themselves and how the precinct Captain had finally treated them with respect and agreed to work with them. The mood was one of celebration.

But the celebration was premature. The Captain refused to answer calls from the group and described their meeting with him as "confrontational" and "disrespectful." Now the group had to take action or return to its previous state of powerlessness. Had they done anything wrong in asking the Captain for direct and timely action? They concluded they had not. A time for public accountability had arrived: the Captain had to be held accountable for his action or lack of it. The Captain's description of the meeting was so distorted that it angered the leaders. It also led to a discussion of the role of confrontation in bringing about change.

A six-week campaign, which included going over the Captain's head to his superiors, led to results. Slowly, the six drug houses were closed by police action. Police patrols in the neighborhood increased. Each step of the way, Jeanne was there at critical times to provide the support the group needed to continue its campaign, never doing for them what they could do for themselves.

Within the congregation, a new sense of community developed. The pastor used the themes of action to inform his sermons. Neighbors now greeted people on the way to church. The leaders felt a new sense of competence and self-confidence. The people had acted on their faith in a way that directly connected their spiritual lives with their and their neighbors' everyday problems. The campaign made faith real.

Had someone come to them in the beginning, in their discouragement over their dwindling numbers, and said, "You must do something substantial about the crime in the neighborhood," or, "It's your Christian responsibility to visit with hundreds of families in the area," would they have done it? Their despair, inertia, lack of skills and sense of powerlessness made such action unlikely. But they had begun by sharing with one another their faith, their own pain and their real concerns—and then had taken logical steps to reach out in wider circles to their neighbors. Beginning with the life experience of the people in the congregation, the organizer helped them construct a believable vision of something they could do that connected their faith to action in the world. The action was too small to make the evening TV news, but for the people who took part in it, it was huge. They actually confronted "the system," and when it refused to respond, they continued the confrontation until they achieved accountability. Had they lost, their experience of failure would have confirmed the common view that "you can't fight City Hall." With their success came the first taste of the power of acting together in reflective, purposeful ways. Using a cycle of action and reflection, "ordinary people" did extraordinary things.

During this period, leaders from the congregation were meeting with and hearing the stories of the other congregations in ACCO, identifying common concerns and experiences. One common experience, regardless of whatever public official was being dealt with, was a response which in effect said, "I'd like to respond, but I can't because people from across town have a bigger need in this area than you do." What the leaders discovered was that "across town" was wherever the officials weren't. Leaders began to recognize that their congregations had to work together if they wanted to achieve responsiveness on larger issues. A larger vision began developing as Latinos, African-Americans and "Anglos" met, told their stories and worked together. Their efforts brought together Catholics and Protestants (in some cities joined by Jews, Muslims, Unitarians and other people of faith). They increasingly saw their diversity as a source of strength. United in a common faith in a God of justice and compassion and in a new vision of the capacity of religious bodies, they were learning to act skillfully and powerfully in the midst of darkness and despair to bring change in the world.

The victory in closing the drug houses was only the beginning of a process of community building and congregational renewal. The insulated family feeling that characterized New Life Church was being discarded for the challenge of reaching out—to one another and to neighbors—engaging and acting on shared concerns, and in the process, deepening faith.

This process also brought painful organizational changes. As in most, in this congregation a relatively small group of people had held most of the positions of church authority and did most of the work. While they complained, they also made it difficult for new people to be part of real decision-making in congregation life. They would have to change or be pushed aside by a new leadership with a commitment to growth and faith-based action. Such change is difficult, requiring patience and leadership from the pastor and other respected people within a church. At New Life, the old guard resisted. Having lamented the absence of new people, some of the old guard decided they didn't want them if it meant this kind of action. A struggle ensued. The old guard wanted the church to withdraw from ACCO, but failed in their effort to pull the congregation out of the larger community organization. An emerging new leadership, joined by some of the older leaders who liked what was happening, rose to the occasion. The internal struggle over the character of the congregation took two years. Even with a change in pastor, the old guard could not regain control.

Many congregations fail to function as communities. Members come to worship services as "consumer members"—not as co-creators. There is little challenge of one another—instead a polite, "how's it going?" style predominates. Perhaps the pastor serves as a counselor when people are in trouble and pain, but there is little real sharing of people's core concerns.

Congregations that become active in organizing often discover new dimensions of their faith as they reach out to neighbors and involve them in common struggle against the "principalities and powers." In the process, relationships with neighbors deepen. This approach calls on the congregation to take a special kind of responsibility for its neighborhood. It is the responsibility to activate one's neighbors, challenging them to shift from passivity to participation and to move from victimhood and powerlessness to self-empowerment. The goal is not simply to provide services (though in some circumstances these may be appropriate), nor to speak in their behalf. Instead, organizing involves a relationship-building process in which members of the congregation act in community with local residents, becoming partners, friends and real neighbors.

Members of the congregation will also invite unchurched neighbors to share a worship service. If the church provides a spiritual home, they will join. Thus church growth and mission become two sides of the same coin.

The story of New Life is about the beginning of a deeper community. People listened to determine deep concerns; reached out and involved most members of the congregation, and further reached out to their neighbors. They decided to act, made commitments to each other to do the home visits, and held each other accountable for the visits. They learned to both support and challenge one another. They also learned to hold political decision makers accountable for their actions. In their celebration, reflection and evaluation, they learned and grew—deepening their trust in themselves and one another, their faith and their knowledge.

Proverbs says, "Without a vision, the people perish." In these times, many people are perishing. The question is whether religious congregations will build the kinds of communities that offer hope. Those that do will both grow and be true to their faith.

The story of New Life Church was repeated across ACCO, as it has been repeated throughout the country in different places including Catholic, Protestant, Muslim, Unitarian, Jewish, Mormon, Buddhist and other faith communities, drawing together African-Americans, Latinos, Anglos, Asians, and more. An "organizing plan" is tailored for each to the particularities of the congregation and its context. To a much lesser extent, other kinds of voluntary associations are becoming involved in such renewal efforts—unions, parent, tenant and homeowner organizations, and others.

In most of the American City congregations, people had experience with surveys and censuses, or with home evangelism visits. But never had they sought to uncover common concerns with their neighbors and invite these neighbors to participate with congregation members in action they would decide on and take together. The leadership groups that developed in most of the congregations were a mix of members and others.

In fact, it turned out that some of the neighbors had once been members—particularly in some of the Catholic parishes. For example, when the relatively new priest in another Catholic Church in ACCO opened one of the church-neighborhood meetings in his parish hall, he said, "It's good to have so many non-Catholics here with us this evening." A quiet tittering followed his remark. After the meeting, he asked one of his parish leaders what he said that had been funny. "Most of the people there were parish members," she told him. "They just haven't been around for quite a while." The church was now doing something that affected their families, and they wanted to be part of it.

The central problem facing organizers is how to shift people from non-participation to participation and to sustain their participation once the shift takes place. In addition to time pressures against such participation, most communities, particularly low-income, minority communities, have a history of defeats which becomes self-reinforcing because it contributes to a culture of disempowerment. Sometimes participation in past activities had created opportunities for a few to move up and out, and for even fewer to administer service, community-development or advocacy programs sponsored by government, corporate, church or foundation sources. For everyone else, the saying, "you can't beat City Hall" remained too true. To overcome this folk wisdom, Jeanne Steuben and her staff had to teach local leaders the art of choosing first issues, thinking through with them how successful action on these first issues related to other issues and allaying their fears of possible conflict and confrontation.

First Issues: Immediate, Specific and Winnable

In her teaching, Jeanne placed major emphasis on the organization as the vehicle for addressing the multiple problems of the community. All the leaders knew family stories of poverty or economic stress and frustration. All of them faced institutional problems. What they constantly had to examine was the relationship of building an organization to all these problems. One of the most important lessons Jeanne had to teach leaders was that problems are actually *opportunities*. They provide openings for building an organization that, as it becomes more powerful, can solve ever more recalcitrant problems—more recalcitrant because there are greater status quo self-interests to overcome to resolve them. At the same time, the experience of working together on common concerns fosters the creation of more meaningful community.

Leaders had thought about what they could do to solve problems, and they had started many service programs as ways to address problems they encountered in the neighborhood. Some had thought about what government or private institutions could do to solve problems and had tried to get politicians, bureaucrats, private owners and managers to adopt policies and programs they thought would improve their community. But they had not thought about how to use problems as opportunities to engage the people affected by those problems in thinking about, deciding upon, and implementing action aimed at solving the problems.

Many of the leaders initially wanted action on a large issue that would unite them in all their splendid diversity. But Jeanne asked how they thought their members would respond if the issue wasn't solved in a year, a question that led to a workshop on the "Criteria for First Issues."

From the point of view of shifting non-participating people to participation—that is from the point of view of organization building—the initial problems tackled must be immediate and specific. Most people don't come to meetings about what will happen ten years from now, nor do they come to meetings about great generalities ("the public schools crisis"). They might come to a meeting about specific things happening in the school their child attends. But proposed solutions to problems must be immediate, specific, winnable, believable, and non-divisive or they won't stick around for long. Hope for change, which inspires participation leading to action, depends on the belief that change is indeed *possible*. At the beginning, especially, people need to experience some success fairly quickly to begin to believe in this possibility. And this requires a careful consideration of the power and time necessary to make particular changes happen.

The New Life Church story, related above, gives a good example of how organizations make these kinds of determinations. Before they engaged in conflict with the local police captain, they decided that a group of fifty to one hundred activated church members and neighborhood residents might be able to generate enough pressure to get him to close a drug house. The issue was theoretically "winnable" and the group's goal was "specific."

Every such effort always involves risk, however. The precinct captain, like any public official, is faced with many other pressures as he decides how he will allocate the scarce resource of police officers. He operates within various constraints—his superiors' expectations, budget limitations, and the demands from citizens in other parts of his precinct. It is likely that he will try to avoid responding positively the first time he meets with a group who wants the drug houses closed; indeed, he may seek to avoid any meeting at all. Simply agreeing to meet is a first acknowledgment of the group, implying recognition of it as a legitimate voice for the concerns of the neighborhood. Once in a meeting, it is difficult to say "no."

But while the captain may have a general concern about the growing alienation of the body politic, as well as a concern about safety in the neighborhood, he also has an immediate concern about his resources—if he "spends" them in one place, he may have to take them from another, at least in the short run, and it is in the short run that he lives: from budget cycle to budget cycle, from departmental meeting to departmental meeting, from one promotional review to the next.

For the community group to assess whether closing the drug house is a winnable issue, then, it must have an idea of what it will do if it initially meets a negative response, and the organization must assess how long it can sustain participation before people return to their previously held belief "you can't beat City Hall." (Private sector decision-makers face similar considerations: what competitors will do; how lenders, investors, suppliers, government regulators and consumers might respond; the effect of a policy on recruiting talent to work for a company; "image" and others.)

Since the decision-maker, in his first encounters with "people power," is typically assessing whether or not to "spend" resources—including money or materials, personnel time, his reputation, and that of his organization—the community organization must be able to make refusal to spend resources costly enough for the decision-maker to decide the wiser course is to negotiate. If the residents launch an imaginative campaign, it will begin to "cost" the decision-maker too much not to negotiate. Reaching agreement may take a couple of months and several public actions.

Having shut one drug house down, a "small victory" they can celebrate and tell others about, the community organization is more likely to be able to convince neighbors on other blocks that if they organize, they can get rid of their drug houses as well.[3]

Initial victories in each of ACCO's congregations progressively increased leaders' self-confidence and skills. Through action, they learned how to: research a problem; come up with "actionable proposals"; negotiate with those who had power to adopt their proposals; and take action when good faith negotiations weren't taking place. Their own experience showed them that larger victories could be won if more people got involved. Some of the people who simply attended a large neighborhood meeting decided they wanted to

---

[3] The answer to the critic who worries that shutting a drug house on one block will simply move it a couple of blocks away is that other neighbors should also organize, and that when organizing spreads the people will be able to tackle more recalcitrant problems with broader solutions.

join the local church-community committees.

Skeptics will not be convinced by words alone. Only results, combined with a reflection on their meaning and evaluation of how they were achieved, will do the convincing. It did not matter that Jeanne knew that 4,000 involved people would be a force in American City, because her knowledge was outside the experience of most of the people living in the area of the drug house and in the other member organizations of ACCO. Even if Jeanne had told the story convincingly, the likely response would have been, "Yeah, but it's different here."

In fact, the most difficult thing a person faces when he begins to get active in an organization is going home and telling a skeptical spouse or neighbor what got accomplished at the meeting. Organizations made up of activists don't have this problem. The activists talk to and support one another. But such organizations also remain isolated from the mainstream of life in the constituencies for whom they want to speak, occasionally "mobilizing" constituents on a hot issue, but losing connection with them when the mobilization is over because no web of continuing relationships is built. Jeanne and her staff used an action/reflection cycle to teach an ever-growing group of leaders how to draw new people into each congregation-community committee. In individual and small group meetings they listened to people, involved them in planning action as well as participation in the crowds that impressed decision-makers that they better take this group seriously.

ACCO's organizing process used small victories to build more participation, and then used larger numbers to gain bigger results. The two are in constant interplay, each strengthening the other.

For example, when crime related issues came up in most of the congregations in ACCO, it was apparent to everyone that local victories were not enough. As a result, during its third year ACCO's leaders decided to tackle the basic approach of the police department. An organization-wide leadership committee made up of seventy-three members conducted hundreds of "research actions" to learn about "community policing." The next year, the organization got 2,000 people to a meeting with police department and local elected officials. It proposed a shift from high technology and cops in cars to an emphasis on "beat cops" and close ties to neighborhoods as the means to control crime. The "cost" of such a shift is high, even if fewer dollars are actually spent in the long run. The proposed reorganization of the police department, calling for a major shift in its way of doing business, ultimately became an issue in the mayoral race. ACCO wanted the "macho cop," insulated from the public by his car, gun and reputation, to give way to a community-sensitive police department. The new mayor claimed to support community policing, and a new police commission was appointed. A leader from the community organization was appointed to the search committee for a new police chief.

Jeanne's insistence that as many congregations as she could convince engage in their own community-building and issue identification process led to the development of leaders in each of the congregations and a congregation-community committee. On small issues, they learned the basics. By the time they met together to form the organization-wide action committee they were already tested. They knew they could count on each other to deliver people because they knew that each had done the painstaking job of reaching out and developing relationships within their own congregation and with their neighbors.[4]

In community organizations across the country, as in American City, residents of drug-infested neighborhoods who started out with "law and order" approaches to limiting drug-use and crime have learned that arrest and conviction are not sufficient to stop crime. They have learned this because of their own study of and experience with the issue. As local leaders become involved, they ask, and are challenged by organizers to ask, questions that get deeper into the matter at hand. Who are the youth who are often the runners for the dealers and themselves dealers? What would it take to get them to stop dealing? Who are the users? What would it take to get them to stop using? Are we prepared to talk with youth leaders who would be willing to talk with us? What are we prepared to do with them and in their behalf? Out of such conversations comes action for jobs, drug rehabilitation programs, improved schools and after-school activities, as well as opportunities for meaningful community roles for youth.

Choosing first issues that were immediate, specific and winnable made sense to local leaders because Jeanne helped them understand that the first issues were stepping stones to other issues that also were of concern to them that they recognized would be more costly to institutional decision-makers to solve. "The organization we are building," Jeanne and her staff kept reminding local leaders, "is not meant to go away after one or another problem is solved. It is meant to stay here, both to monitor what has been won, and to move on to other issues as well."

---

[4] A caveat: in some situations a broadly-based community organization can be initiated with a campaign on a large issue whose impact is so wide, deep, immediate and specific that it demands action. Similarly, in a time of social movement, as during the organization of industrial workers in the 1930s and the civil rights movement in the Deep South in the period 1955-mid 1960s, large issue campaigns—like the right to vote—can be used to build organization. Organizers in this tradition make a sharp distinction between issue mobilization, on the one hand, and organization building, on the other. The two are related, but the distinction between them is largely overlooked or not understood by many activists.

Multi-issue Organizations

When Jeanne met with individual leaders, and when leaders talked with one another in small group meetings or workshops, they heard a wide range of concerns. Young parents were concerned about small children, and those with older children were concerned about high schools and jobs beyond school. In the various meetings, Jeanne kept coming back to the common theme of powerlessness. "We are powerless to deal with these concerns because we don't have a large organization involving significant numbers of people," she would say. The next step in her argument was that "to get people involved, we must begin with their immediate concerns. These will be different from person to person, congregation to congregation, neighborhood to neighborhood. The organization we design must be capable of responding to all of these problems." Obviously, priorities had to be set and criteria for undertaking issues had to be decided upon. But the design of the organization had to be such that everyone could see it both responding to immediate concerns and, if it was successful, responding to larger and longer-range concerns "down the road." In general, because of the wide range of issues people bring to the table, and the importance of building an organization with the widest possible support, broadly-based community organizations are multi-issue in character.

The multi-issue framework also created the possibility of an organization-wide "platform." In its third year, ACCO held an organization-wide meeting to adopt a statement of vision for American City. The statement talked about the health of the city requiring affordable housing, decent jobs for all, opportunities for youth, good schools and child care, the elimination of toxics from apartments and neighborhoods, drug treatment and prevention, and neighborhood safety and security. The statement was accompanied by priority actions the organization resolved to take in the coming year.

A multi-issue community organization becomes a permanent vehicle to express its members' (and their neighbors') interests and values. This permanence is needed to enforce victories that have been won which, over time and in the absence of enforcement, can be eroded. But it is also needed because the broader purpose of these organizations is to democratize public life, to challenge present concentrations of wealth and power, and to create authentic communities of people who are more than consumers.

The organizers worked with local leaders in each of the congregations to identify first issues and set up meetings with the decision-makers who had the authority to act on proposed solutions. Often, local leaders wanted to start with petition campaigns, or have one or two leaders meet with the decision-makers, or ask a local elected official or a lawyer to act in their behalf.

The idea that research actions would identify appropriate decision-makers and that these decision-makers should respond to the people in public meetings was a new one. Each of the possibilities raised by the local leaders had to be reviewed and discussed. Each was an opportunity to return to the dual task of winning issues and building an organization. None of these discussions was more difficult for many of the church people than those that dealt with conflict and confrontation.

Conflict: Personalizing, Polarizing, and Confronting

In the second year, Jeanne hired a local person as a second staff member, and her organizing network placed a "trainee" to work under her supervision. Jeanne and her staff used role-playing to teach and train local leaders as they prepared to meet decision-makers like the precinct captain. In almost all their role-playing sessions the same resistance to framing issues in "yes" or "no" terms occurred. Jeanne predicted that if the issues weren't clearly framed, with no room to wiggle, the groups wouldn't get the answers they hoped for, nor would there be clarity about the responses they were getting. "He won't do that," leaders would say. Or, "we can't stop him from speaking, can we?" Or, "it wouldn't be very polite to do that." Most of the objections were handled in the role playing. Jeanne would play the precinct captain (or whatever official a particular group was going to meet). She would be nice, want to engage in "dialog" with the people and simply refuse to respond to the specifics of their proposals. Sometimes the training sessions would take a couple of hours. But finally the point became clear to the leaders: the proposals being made were legitimate, and the people wanted specific answers.

There is much talk these days of "new partnerships," "win-win," "getting to 'yes'," and similar consensus approaches to resolving disagreements between groups. These approaches fail to recognize the power dimension of political and economic life. When people who wield power embark on a new course, they must be very secure and very powerful and thus not constrained by the threat of rivals and competitors. Or, they must see that the price paid to maintain the status quo is not worth paying. In the latter case, politicians measure the price by seeing how many potential voters are involved. Private business owners might look at the number of potential boycotters involved with its impact on profit, or damage to reputation—and therefore recruitment of talent. In both cases, they are at least partly concerned about their reputation, about their "good standing" in the city.

As a result, one should expect decision-makers in the public or private sector to test demands made upon them by the previously powerless. Are there really consequences for inaction? They must determine if the costs of conceding to group demands outweigh the benefits. As we come to understand this, we learn to embrace non-violent conflict as the partner of change, as a necessary precursor to agreement. Complete intransigence from the opposition usually arises either because of an unyielding commitment to maintaining the status quo, or out of a desire to eliminate the power of a new voice seeking recognition at the negotiating table. It does not arise as a natural outcome of conflict.

In fact, what the powerless generally fail to understand is that those in power are *often* engaged in conflict. Conflict, of one form or another, is a natural condition for the maintenance of power in a world where different interests often struggle for control. Most powerful people know how to deal with conflict. Most are used to dealing with conflict. It is the powerless who see conflict as somehow uncivilized. Decision-makers know this, and often seek to use this sense of misplaced politeness to control.

When the powerless seek a place at the decision-making table, they assert the right to be there. If the claim is ignored or denied, they must demonstrate their power. It was not the Precinct Captain with whom New Life dealt who "empowered" them; rather it was their effort in their own behalf that made it possible for them to be at the table, and it was that effort that made them confident of why they were there. It is fashionable these days to speak of "empowering" others, but if we look carefully at what is meant, such empowerment is usually limited to the role of participant in a program designed and controlled by someone else. An organization seated at the decision-making table without struggle can just as easily be unseated if those who brought it to the table change their minds, or if new decision-makers emerge who want different people seated.

Meetings with officials are the means by which community organizations seek agreements. When such officials refuse to meet or, when meeting, refuse to engage in good faith negotiations, a necessary confrontation arises between the previously powerless and those with authority to reach agreements with them. The alternative is to return home and admit that what was sought wasn't legitimate after all, or to say, "We got beat...."

When there are contradictory views, there is disagreement. When disagreements are pressed, there is confrontation, and with confrontation there is polarization. Polarization clarifies issues—and even makes the word "issue" itself clear. There is no issue if there is no controversy. There is agreement, thus not an issue; or there is a problem with no one to effectively speak in behalf of those suffering it.

It is important to emphasize that disagreements are inevitably with *people* who can make decisions—not with buildings that are picketed or "The System" which is denounced. Conflicts over issues are personalized because proposals for change are made to *individuals* who represent organized interests, not to abstractions. A group doesn't meet with "the system." One of Jeanne Steuben's favorite challenges to leaders who feared personal confrontation was to ask, "Did you notice how, when Jesus dealt with the moneylenders in the Temple, he politely said, 'Excuse me gentlemen, would you mind moving your tables?'" Of course, everyone laughed.....and thought.

Those who act with power often prefer fuzziness; I call it "mush". Without clarity, it is difficult to mobilize the righteous anger of otherwise tame, disorganized, and oppressed people. In fact, corporations send their public relations personnel to training sessions where they are taught to "fog" an issue; politicians and bureaucrats are adept at doing the same thing.

Consequently, organizers spend hours in role-playing sessions with leaders to prepare them to pierce the fog—i.e. for the various techniques that are likely to be used by those they encounter in positions of power. They teach leaders to ask clear, "yes or no" questions—like those asked of the police captain in the first example.

After one such role-playing session in which an organizer played the mayor of a large American city, a delegation of some thirty leaders of the organization met with the mayor. Some of his words were exactly those used by the organizer in the role-playing session. Afterward, there was a noticeable coolness on the part of many of the leaders toward their organizer. "What's going on?" he asked. There was hesitation, but the relationship of trust between leaders and organizer was deep. One of the leaders asked, "did you talk with the mayor about this meeting before we met him?" The organizer was surprised by the question, and said, "No, why do you ask?" "He sounded just like you when you role-played him." The truth is that they more or less say the same things. When the organizer told the leaders that, they all laughed and went on with the post-meeting evaluation.

Meetings with "Decision-Makers"

Almost everything Jeanne had to teach came together in the preparation for meetings with "decision-makers," the meetings themselves, and the post-meeting evaluation. The drama of a three-act play unfolds, with heroes and villains, the uncertainty of how the plot will unfold, the high point of tension, and the final resolution.

By "decision-makers," organizers mean those people to whom a proposal for action might appropriately be made. You don't propose to the street cleaning department that it improve bus service, and you don't propose to the utility company that it make better home appliances or stop selling poor quality produce in the neighborhood store.

It is now common practice for initial encounters to be "research meetings" or "research actions". A delegation from the community organization wants to meet with a wide variety of people whose decisions bear on a problem the community organization is addressing. For example, if they're concerned about affordable housing, they might be meeting with appropriate decision-makers in the urban renewal agency, the city planning and zoning departments, the Federal Department of Housing and Urban Development, private development companies, private landlords or property management companies, the public housing authority, banks or savings and loan institutions, the mayor or someone in his office, and others they determine might have authority to do something that would affect affordable housing. From these meetings, the community organization will develop a series of "proposals" to place on the table before a decision-maker who can address the problem of insufficient or inadequate affordable housing.

Research would also determine the points of vulnerability of these decision-makers, because the community organization is interested in "next steps" in case they are unable to come to a mutually satisfactory agreement. The ultimate sanction available to the community organization is its capacity to bring pressure to bear on a decision-maker sufficient to bring him or her to an agreement with the organization. The forms of pressure are many. For politicians, they have to do with denying votes, volunteers, or contributions. For a private business, they have to do with profits and a public image that might affect profits and recruitment of talent. For a public bureaucracy, they have to do with stability, future appropriations, the reputation of an executive director, or what a politically appointed board of directors or politicians might do.

In each case, possible tactics range from public mass meetings in which commitments are sought from decision-makers (with consequences if they aren't given), to disruptive public action, to boycotts, to lobbying, voter education/ registration/get-out-the-vote drives.

From these two kinds of research, a strategy will emerge. A red-lining savings and loan association that is seeking to buy another savings and loan company, for example, is vulnerable to a public action with the governmental agency that must approve the buy-out. An association that isn't vulnerable to regulatory intervention might be subject to the massive withdrawal of funds from religious institutions and their allies who have deposits there. A link to the public arena might be made if it is determined that the city does some kind of business with the association—the organization might threaten to put a proposal to a mayor, city council or board of supervisors to withdraw the public's business from this company which is acting against the public good. A large and powerful organization will be able to extend the scope of the conflict to include many actors in public life—whether from the public or private sectors—pressing the question: "Where do you stand on this issue—with the common good or with private greed?" And so on.

If Americans are to be aroused to participate in their democratic heritage, there will have to be confrontations with people who have power. Decision-makers in public and private institutions responsible for allowing and participating in the abuses of concentrated wealth and power will have to change their ways or be replaced. Institutions that concentrate wealth and power will have to be reorganized and made accountable to the common good.

It is common for community organizations to say confrontation was useful, but they now have moved from conflict to partnership. Nowhere that I've been is there: an end of homelessness, good jobs with good pay for everyone who can work, adequate schools, child care, after-school programs and health care, affordable decent, safe and sanitary housing or healthy environments. Nor am I aware of any place where deliberative assemblies of the citizenry have replaced the politics of polling, marketing, mass media and big money. Rather, politics and the economy remain contested terrain.

Where there is injustice, when an organization says, "we no longer have to struggle for what we want," they are simply admitting that they don't want to struggle for what rightfully should be enjoyed by the people they represent, or that they don't have the power to get what they want and don't want to get that power, or that they have joined the existing power structure. They have been co-opted. They are now junior partners in an establishment that skillfully uses concessions, status, patronage and grants as means to absorb dissent and dampen aspirations.

The illusion of the junior partner is often expressed in the phrase, "we have won respect and equality at the bargaining table."

Not quite.

When vast political and economic inequalities exist between the parties at the table, the struggle is not over. Rather, the forms of conflict have changed. If the community organization is to remain true to itself, a constant struggle over prerogatives takes place. The post World War II labor movement deluded itself with the idea that it had won respect and equality at the negotiating table. Its "partners" fed the delusion—appointment to various civic committees, civic "honors," access to one another on private phone lines, addressing each other on a first name basis, and a host of other status symbols. Little wonder that today labor has so little power.

The tactics of confrontation need not, indeed should not, be crazy. It is a measure of how media-oriented we have become that we think of a small, screaming, and outrageously rhetorical group as "militant," while massive numbers of people engaged in a boycott, public accountability session or electoral activity are seen as "moderate."

The test of tactics is two-fold:

- First, a tactic should contribute toward winning.
- Second, and equally important, any tactic should contribute to building an organization. That is, it should directly involve more people in active roles within the organization, deepen the skills and self-confidence of leaders, recruit new allies and members, and broaden the organization's appeal to the wider public.

In confrontations, the arrogance of power often exposes itself. This leads regular people to do what they didn't imagine themselves doing before. To quote Alinsky's classic phrase, "the action is in the reaction."

When New Life Church and its neighbors met with the Precinct Captain, he said "yes" to their proposals. Afterward he refused to implement them and described the meeting in a way its church and community participants felt was a distortion. It made people mad. That anger could have been turned on one another. It could have led to recrimination and self-recrimination. It could have led to scapegoating another group. It could have led people to say, "see, we can't beat City Hall." But Jeanne Steuben's role was to find ways to channel the anger into a constructive next action step. Because their role playing had anticipated various outcomes of the meeting, ranging from the Captain not coming to his saying "yes," the eighteen member leadership core group was prepared. Jeanne's challenging questions helped them direct their anger outward in responsible action congruent with the group's values.

When anger informs thoughtful action, it is liberating for powerless people. When it does not, it becomes what Langston Hughes called "a dream deferred." And dreams deferred, as we have painfully learned, too often end in drugs, gangs, crime and riots—the a-political politics of the powerless—or, more typically, in demoralization and despondency.

None of this is to say that community organizations shouldn't be in partnerships with the powerful. Real negotiations lead to solutions to problems. The object of action is real negotiations. But the job of negotiations doesn't end with one campaign or issue. Indeed, the relationships of mutual respect that can result from such engagements may persuade adversaries to become allies, demonstrate that a different path can benefit most or all parties to a dispute, and even persuade former opponents that things are fundamentally wrong with the current order.

Effective community organizations, then, learn to leave room for adversaries to "save face." The goal is usually not to eliminate opposition. Rather it is to change practices, policies and structures whose effects are unjust or dysfunctional.

Money

At all the workshops local leaders attended before Jeanne Steuben arrived in American City, and in their subsequent conversations, they were confronted with the money question. "Who is going to own the organization?" And, "Can you own the organization if it's someone else's money?"

Pastors who had depended on denominational money knew what it meant to be on "mission status." Those from the smaller churches were frightened by the prospect of a minimum $1,000 dues. Larger congregations faced the challenge of $6,000 or more. Leaders negotiated with one another a formula to determine dues, taking into account membership size, local giving, and total budgets. Jeanne promised that they would learn how to increase the giving of their members in the course of their participation in the organization. In fact, subsequent experience showed that leaders in ACCO could also be called on to be leaders of a congregation fund-raiser or annual pledge drive, increasing giving far beyond dues to ACCO.

The initial funds to hire Jeanne Steuben came chiefly from denominational and a few foundation sources, though local congregations contributed. (A limited number of religious and foundation sources provide funding to seed the development of such organizations.) But these sources expect local fundraising to provide ongoing support. Dues were part of the concept of membership in ACCO from its inception, with the understanding they would grow each of the first three years. The challenge and the objective became to raise the core budget "from the bottom up." ACCO's core budget was $250,000, and provided for three organizers. The core budgets of such organizations typically range from $120,000 to $250,000 and are raised by a combination of dues and an annual "ad book" or raffle. The money primarily pays for the staff of professional organizers and continuing education activities for the voluntary leadership.

To the extent that core budgets require foundation grants, they suffer from the same problems as other kinds of dependency. Jeanne insisted that leaders of the organization deal with religious bodies and foundations. While she wrote the first "boilerplate" proposals, she soon found people within the member congregations who were able to re-write and modify the boilerplate to fit the specific guidelines of individual funding agencies. Her purpose was two-fold. She wanted leadership to understand and operate all aspects of the organization. And, she knew the more the leaders had to deal with the difficulties of foundation fundraising, the more likely they would be to raise money from the membership. Organizations that don't develop stable, internally generated, sources for their core budget find their organizing work increasingly determined by the interests of funding sources.

When members control their organization and are growing in their capacity to address concerns of deep importance to them they will pay for the organization and engage in fundraising activities to keep it alive. An effective measure of member "ownership" of community organizations is to see how the money is raised and by whom. A good operational indicator of whether the members own the organization (and raise funds to pay for their staff) or whether the staff owns it (and raises money to pay its salaries) is to see who actually does the fundraising. "Grassroots money" raised by professional canvassers (or organizers) or by direct mail is not an indication of member ownership any more than paying taxes is an indication that the people control the government. Dues and "bottom-up" member-based fundraising are the surest guarantors of organizational independence and "ownership" by the people themselves.

Reflection, Education, and Celebration

Broad-based community organizations are about institutional change. But that is not all. Democratic power is only developed by the development of democratic citizens. Democratic organizations grow as ever-larger numbers of people develop civic competence and the confidence that they can effectively act on their values and interests. Many organizers define the heart of their work as the development of leaders. Institutional change will follow from that development, but the focus of the work of these organizers is on the development of people.

Increased focus has also been placed on strengthening particular local organizations (usually congregations but sometimes union locals, civic groups and other voluntary associations) and on building deeper communities. One of the results is that community organizations are developing longevity. The conscious introduction of reflection on deeply held values has strongly contributed to these changes.

Connecting community action to religious faith is a powerful experience. When that connection is made, people are not only addressing a local issue, they are also acting as Jesus (or Moses or Mohammed) would have them act. When such a connection is made, the lives of local congregation leaders and members become more significant in their eyes and in the eyes of their families and friends. Jeanne was insistent that reflection on values accompany action, sometimes preceding it, sometimes following it, and sometimes taking place both before and after action. She wanted the leaders to be able to integrate their visits with each other and their neighbors and their action regarding the drug houses with what they believed most deeply. She was struck by the difficulty some of the clergy had in making these connections and she actively pressed the clergy in this regard. Many of them lacked the tools to do this integration. In a "clergy caucus" organized within ACCO, mini-Bible (and in other organizations Torah, Koran, and other sources of faith) study sessions took place in which concepts like power, confrontation, leadership and conflict were examined. Theology took on a new vitality. Pastors and religious education workers began to incorporate themes that came from the clergy caucus meetings into worship and Bible study groups, as well as into reflections at organizing meetings. Stories of what local people were doing were related to stories of courage and action in the Bible. The result was a deepening of faith.

As individual faith became more connected to action on important issues, the faith community itself became more important to them. Their congregation became a place where they could act on values of caring, sharing and justice in ways directly connected to the pressures they, their families and neighbors were experiencing. The telling of stories to and with one another was the means to deepen relationships among them. The deepening of faith in community increased commitment to both the local congregation and to ACCO.

In the best current practice, time is spent connecting what local organizations are doing to their faith and values. Organizers and leaders ask people to reflect on what the Bible, Torah, Koran, Bill of Rights, Declaration of Independence, or other important texts call them to be and do, and to how what they are doing is in their tradition. Unions and civic associations have their own particular additional sources for reflection, often found in the preamble to their constitution. Often religious and secular traditions have joined together, using as reflection material the American Revolution and Bill of Rights, the Abolitionists and the struggle against slavery, the Suffragettes and women's movement, the Knights of Labor and the Populist Movement, the struggle to organize industrial workers in the 1930s, the civil rights movement of the 1960s, contemporary movements for social and economic change, and more.

Most Americans subscribe to the nation's democratic principles. Connecting people's action to their democratic traditions gives them the sense of carrying on what others did before them. A community organization that offers these opportunities allows local people to become heroes—in their own eyes, as well as in the eyes of their children, spouses and neighbors. African-Americans in the black churches in ACCO who thought they needed a Martin Luther King, Jr. to be their leader saw that they could have some of King within themselves. This experience is a powerful antidote to the kind of politics that markets candidates and asks people to depend on a single leader. When local people take risks in the name of what they believe, they are doing more than pursuing an immediate narrow interest. They begin to think in different ways. A different understanding of who makes history emerges for the most active people in a community organization. While the "big leaders" may be important, they really express what thousands of lesser known people are saying; they are standing on the shoulders of thousands of people who make them look tall.

Distinct from reflection, though related to it, is the increasing use of more formal education within community organizations. Organizing rooted in democratic traditions, and the social and economic justice teachings of the world's great religions, seeks to develop a sense of being part of the whole, of having responsibility beyond the self and immediate family, or even immediate neighborhood and city. But organizers part from traditional "educators" in their insistence that moving people toward a deeper understanding and appreciation of democratic citizenship, requires an "educator" to "begin where people are," "start with their experience," and engage them on their own concerns. Organizing provides the context for education; group action is the vehicle to engage people in learning. Many organizers previously assumed that this education was an automatic process, or that one only did it informally in a conversation in a home, coffee shop or bar. Current organizing practice is beginning to incorporate reading, study and engagement with major intellectual issues into its work. For example, Jeanne Steuben and some of her leaders went to network educational sessions in which discussion of Cornel West's *Race Matters* was a major agenda item.

Broadly-based community organization leaders and members throughout the country can tell stories of people coming into their organization because of an immediate concern affecting them, getting to know people of different racial or ethnic groups in that organization, and then discovering that their stereotypes of "The Other" didn't fit their new experiences. Similarly, men who never thought they would accept women's equality found themselves in organizations in which women played key leadership roles. Such situations of "cognitive dissonance" provide "teachable moments" to be used by an organizational leadership that is committed to democratic values. Challenges to prejudices can be made because the participants in the situation are perplexed that their experience and previously held beliefs are not "in sync." While all prejudices don't simply go away, the organization creates situations in which prejudices can be challenged. When asked about earlier racist and classist views, "Anglos" in such organizations often say, "that was before I got to know the people I'm working with now, and had a chance to really think about what I most believed. I also found out that when we weren't working together, we were divided by those who wanted to keep us apart so they could keep things in their control."

Any good community organization is a school without walls. It engages people in civic life and teaches them the skills to negotiate with power. However, engagement alone is not sufficient for people to place their own circumstances in an historical, sociological, political or economic context. Connecting the particular local experience to the broader issues of American democracy requires patience, insight and skill, particularly with leaders who may have high school or less formal education. And the more formally educated may have to unlearn what textbooks taught them. The experiential lessons of organizing, central as they may be, don't inherently lead to understanding larger social structures, their role in perpetuating social problems, or the need to change them.

If organizing is to do more than give one more group a slightly larger piece of the economic or public services pie, or substitute one set of oppressors for another, this kind of education must go on. If the exercise of power is all that sustains involvement, the emerging community organization will simply replicate in its internal workings the systems of domination and hierarchy in the world around it. One need only look at the evolution of the industrial union movement from the 1930s to the 1950s to see this happen. On the other hand, if the use of power is circumscribed and guided by deeply held faith and values, and a deepening appreciation of democratic traditions and practice, there might be the possibility of building power that is collegial and broadly shared, in which those with the most experience are also those who most want to teach what they know to others. That kind of leadership, described by those in the Christian tradition as "servant leadership" and by others as "democratic," may be emerging in the current generation of community organizations. If so, it is in part because these organizations engage in an ongoing interplay between action, reflection and education.

I have found that leaders *want* to learn the workings of the power structures we live within and about how they came to be. Rather than a diversion, as some organizers think, such education deepens organizational commitment because it, like reflection on faith and values, increases the meaning of organizational participation. Similarly, the historical study of those who sought to bring the country closer to its democratic promise in past social movements broadens people and deepens commitment as they learn from both their strengths and shortcomings.

"Organizing is teaching," writes veteran IAF organizer Richard Harmon. "Obviously, not academic-type teaching, which is confined for the most part to stuffing data into people's ears. Organizing is teaching which rests on people's life experiences, drawing them out, developing trust, going into action, disrupting old perceptions of reality, developing group solidarity, watching the growth of confidence to continue to act, then sharing in the emotional foundation for continual questioning of the then-current *status quo*...This means that education is primarily in the *action*, but becomes really liberating education only if the person develops the discipline to rigorously reflect on that action...We have to *own* the questions in this educational process. It must be *our* curiosity that is the engine...pulling us into action, then reflection, then more action, more reflection." In the best current practice, time is deliberately set aside to talk about ideas and their relationship to the reality in which people find themselves.

Finally, we need to celebrate who we are, and to sustain and create culture through storytelling, song, theater, and writing as we build community organizations rooted in a culture of community and solidarity. The labor movement of the 1930s knew this; so did the mid-1950s to mid-1960s southern civil rights movement, and the farm workers union movement. In the skits performed by often self-taught actors and actresses in all these settings, ridicule and humor were used to ease people into the struggle they faced in dangerous and oppressive situations. Singing was part of liberation. In the deepest, darkest, most discouraging moments in the voter registration and community organizing in the Mississippi Delta, where I worked as a SNCC field secretary, we would break into song. As we sang, we believed, and as we believed, we acted. The sharing of common words in song let us know we shared a deeper purpose as well. Every great social movement has created its own literature, theater and music. Community organizing has yet to do that.

Current organizing practice has just begun to tap the power of reflection, education and celebration. It has much to learn from the industrial union movement of the 1930s, the southern civil rights movement during the mid-1950s to mid-1960s, and the farm workers union of the 1960s and 1970s.

In its early years, into the 1970s, community organizing was criticized by some as lacking analysis of interconnections among issues and the power structure. Critics also decried a failure to participate in campaigns that went beyond the local arena.

While they acknowledged the legitimacy of some of these challenges, community organizers working in the tradition described herein stayed true to their analysis. They were uninterested in what has been called "gesture politics"—speaking out on something you lack the power to really do anything about, or decrying a power structure while not have the people power to successfully challenge it.

At the same time, institution/faith-based community organizing increasingly sought to address "the big issues." But the change has not been unambiguous. Questions remain: Can they win victories on this larger level? And, even if they can, can they also enforce those victories? Even more fundamentally, can they democratize the relations of power and challenge undemocratic power more fundamentally?

Can national campaigns be undertaken while at the same time deepening and expanding involvement at the base—which is central to building meaningful people power? Can lobbying of Congress be done in such a way that the mass participation of local accountability sessions can be retained? Can targeting of multi-national corporations or financial institutions be done in a way that continues to involve large numbers of people? And can it open the question of what the country (and world) are going to do with private power that is so big it defines public life?

These are some of the questions now discussed and debated by the organizers and leaders of congregation-based community organizing. For my part, I hope for bolder initiatives that seize the opportunity that exists in the present economic crisis that grips the country and world. The early Occupy Wall Street demonstrations, and the support they received from a wide range of Americans, show the possibilities that might exist. Congregation-based, and other, community organizing constitutes one of the hopeful signs of our times.

Teaching Politics as If It Matters

Introduction

For the past forty-plus years, I have been a community organizer, working with religious, labor, interest, identity and issue groups. As my work continued, I sought to systematize a way to introduce people to aspects of political and sociological theory—i.e. how do citizens, potential citizens, residents of a place, workers, unemployed people, welfare recipients, pastors and others answer the question, "How do I understand the world in which I am living?" I use a highly interactive workshop in which I ask a lot of questions, and workshop participants supply the answers. The sequence of the questions is connected with what workshop participants are doing in their community (or labor) organizations, and builds on scenarios that are familiar to them in their own organizational work. What follows typically takes three hours of a four-day workshop.

The workshop begins with these questions, "How do we move people from inaction to engagement?" "How can you unite a broad constituency behind an action program?" "How do low-to-middle income people who range on a tactical spectrum from moderates-to-militants and on an ideological or political spectrum from conservatives to radicals, with liberals and independents in the middle, work together to achieve significant change? I use the word "radical" to mean getting at the root of things. The root of the things dealt with in this workshop is, on the one hand, the power of dominant political, economic and cultural institutions, and, on the other, the present personal and community powerlessness felt by many combined with the capacity for powerful action that exists in everyday people and their communal institutions. Earlier in the workshop participants elaborated upon the values to guide action as those of the major social and economic justice teachings of the religious traditions of the world and the secular small "d" democratic tradition.

Theory

The first step in this workshop session is to ask, "What are the problems you want to address in your organization?" All kinds of things are said in response, ranging from "overcrowding at 'X' elementary School," "a $50.00 a month rent increase in my building," to "people in my church don't earn enough at their jobs to make ends meet," "people in my neighborhood are unemployed," or even more general, like "unemployment," "poor quality education," "affordable housing." Some people will identify things like "racism," "sexism," "discrimination" and "prejudice." Others will say things like "rent control," "community control of schools," a "job training and motivation programs." These are all written on a chalkboard or easel pad.

I then draw lines around the lists so they are in four groupings,

Group 1	Group 2	Group 3	Group 4
$50 rent increase in my building	Unemployment	racism prejudice	rent control
overcrowding at 'X' school	Quality education	sexism classism	community control
	Affordable housing		job training and motivation programs

and ask, "What do the items in each group share in common, and what distinguishes them from the other three groups?" This discussion takes a while, perhaps ten to twenty minutes. I want it to. I then add the following to each of the groups as headings or words to categorize what is in the list and ask if the group headings are acceptable:

Group 1	Group 2	Group 3	Group 4
"problems,"	"topics"	"analyses"	"solutions" or "possible solutions"

Typically these words have already been used by people in the workshop. After some discussion, in all but one (I'll return to this one in a minute) of the many workshops I've done there is agreement on these categories and brief definitions or explanations I propose for each:

- A problem is specific; it is something people experience.
- A topic is general.
- Analyses seek to explain why things are as they are.

- Solutions or proposed solutions seek to diminish or eliminate problems.

"If you want to get people who feel powerless to a meeting, where do you start?" There is agreement that you have to start with their problems, not general topics or analyses. Put in organizing terms, "start with where people are, not where you'd like them to be."

"Why do people have these problems?" This is a question that also leads to lots of responses: "the power structure," "racism" (or any of the other isms), "unemployed people are lazy" (or lack motivation, or are untrained), "politicians don't care" (or are owned by the people who pay for their campaigns), "the school district is incompetent," "teachers are inadequate," "the people downtown are screw-ups," "some people just don't care," "it's always been this way, and always will be this way," "landlords just want to make a buck," and the list continues.

I do a similar grouping of ideas on my working space,

Group 1	Group 2	Group 3
• The power structure • racism • sexism • classism • other isms • incompetent screw ups	The unemployed are: • untrained • unmotivated • lazy Students are: • unmotivated • lazy Parents don't care	It's always been this way, and always will be this way.

and ask people to give me words to categorize the groups. I write what they say on the workspace.

I then ask if these categories (some of which they may already have come up with) include everything they've said:

Fault of the system	Fault of the person	In the nature of things. Ordained by God.

Whenever I've done this, people agree that these problems exist or persist either because of the "fault of the people" with the problems, or the "fault of the system" that has the authority and resources to solve the problems, or a combination of the two. A simple example might be that tenants didn't take care of their apartments or the landlord ignored problems of maintenance and repairs or a combination of the two.

Sometimes people say the problems are inevitable, to which I respond, "if you think all these problems can't be solved, that they are in the nature of things or ordained by God, then you are in the wrong workshop." That always brings a laugh. (While that kind of fatalism isn't common in the United States, there are other places in the world that it is.)

"Do we agree that to the extent a problem is the "fault" of the system, then the system has to change, and to the extent it is the "fault" of the person experiencing it, then the person has to change?" Again, my experience has been that workshop participants agree that to the extent a problem is the fault of the people experiencing the problem, then the people have to change, and to the extent it is the fault of the system, then the system has to change. Changing the people includes things like training, counseling, motivation, education or even psychotherapy. And, participants acknowledge the source of at least some part of some problems is "the system."

I then ask, "Can we agree that by 'the system' we mean a combination of values, institutions that embody or put into practice these values, and decision-makers who occupy key positions in these institutions?"

I then say, "we're now going to look at that portion of a problem or problems that results from something "the system" is or isn't doing, (no one doubts that at least some portion of some problems is systemic in nature) and ask, "Why don't the decision-makers fix the problems?" Again after discussion and categorizing ideas there is agreement that if the system isn't solving a problem that it could solve, the reason is:

- it doesn't know about it,
- it is incompetent, or
- it has different interests.

I then ask questions designed to determine what strategy follows from each of these explanations for why the system doesn't solve problems. "If the system doesn't know, what do you do?" Agreement emerges that if the system doesn't know about the problem, then the strategy for change is to educate or inform the system (specifically, its decision-makers). If the system is incompetent, then the strategy that follows is to train the system's personnel, restructure it or replace it. If the system isn't solving problems because it is guided by different interests, then the strategy for change would be to change its interests, change the system or create an alternative system.

We agreed that at least in some instances, and to some extent, some problems exist because something we have agreed to call "the system" or "the power structure" has an interest in keeping things the way they are, in preserving the status quo. That interest might have to do with money, status, power or some combination of all of these.

In all my 40+ years of organizing, I only once had the experience of a workshop participant refusing to accept this framework. In this case, an African-American woman insisted that racism was a problem that was experienced, not simply an analysis that explained things like discrimination in employment, red-lining of neighborhoods, overcrowded schools in inner cities and so forth. In that case, I said "o.k. we're going to stipulate that you disagree with the definitions we're giving to words here. Is it o.k. if the rest of us go on with our agreements?" She let us proceed. We later had a long conversation over a break and she stuck by her guns. I still don't understand why, but I know she didn't do much organizing or providing leadership in a low-income Black neighborhood or church. She was working on a PhD at the time.

In a few circumstances, I've had workshop participants who say the system is so hopelessly inadequate that all that can be done is to create alternatives to it. Those who deal with the day-to-day experiences of tenants with bad landlords, parents whose kids are in bad schools, people without health care, un- or under-employed people, or people with bad employers, and the myriad of other problems confronting everyday people simply aren't persuaded that you can walk away from these problems and build alternatives. Nor, on the grander scale of discussion, do they want to leave the present system in the hands of people who could bring about global war or ecological disaster. It is not that alternative institutions shouldn't be part of the arsenal of change. Rather, it is that they cannot be the only arrow in the quiver.

Conservatives, libertarians, moderates, centrists, liberals, progressives and radicals who participated in these workshops agreed on this step-by-step approach to how to understand the world. The conservatives thought "the fault of the people" was generally the reason for problems. The radicals thought "the fault of the system."

To the extent that a problem was the fault of the system, people on the center-to-right end of the political spectrum emphasized that it was because the system didn't know about the problem; others, now including some liberals, acknowledged that possibility but emphasized the incompetence of the system; some liberals and the radicals acknowledged what had already been said but emphasized different self-interests of the system. Some of them thought you could change the interests of the system; others thought you had to change the system as a whole or create an alternative system—which in this context meant new or parallel institutions such as alternative schools or cooperatives, or taking or using "state power" to, for example, expropriate a business or create a new system. This would sometimes become the subject of heated debates that I would let continue for a while before taking the workshop participants to a next step.

Role-playing is an extraordinarily powerful teaching tool, one that I always use in teaching this particular material. The workshop would agree to use a specific problem as an example to illustrate what we were discussing. Often we would use the example of a landlord who had raised the rent in his building 25% with no changes in his maintenance, repair or other costs. We would stipulate that he had good tenants because we were illustrating changing the system, not changing the people. I would then tell the group that I was going to play the landlord and would give them time to prepare themselves to negotiate with me.

Two kinds of lessons are learned in this role playing. One set of lessons had to do with how you organize yourselves to present a proposed change to a decision-maker; that's not what I want to talk about here. (The other set of lessons is below in "Conflict Tactics.")

There are also important political theory lessons to be teased out of this role-play. The radicals and liberals agree that it is logically possible that the landlord didn't know the hardships being caused by a 25% increase in rent, and that since there are conservatives and centrists in the group with whom they wanted to remain united they would go along with "the landlord doesn't know" as a beginning assumption. That meant telling stories about the hardship such a rent increase imposed on otherwise good tenants. But, those who were skeptical of this theory said, "if it turns out that after we tell the landlord the hardships and he doesn't budge an inch then you centrists and conservatives have to be willing to look at a different explanation for his behavior." The conservatives and centrists had to agree.

I then played the role of an affluent landlord who simply wanted to maximize the profit he could get from his building, saying things like, "I'm sure you can find cheaper housing if you move out of San Francisco," or "you don't have to live here if you don't want to. I know there are people who would pay the additional 25% for these apartments." At some point it was evident to everyone in the room that I wasn't going to budge and that my interest was maximizing the profit I could make from my building. I was increasing the rent not because I didn't know the problem the rent hike posed for my good tenants, but because I had a different interest— maximizing the immediate income I could generate from my building. If self-interest was guiding why the landlord was acting this way and saying these things, a different approach was required. And a strategy followed.

The catalyst for radical (i.e. going to the root) education in this situation is what landlords said and did. Many of the people who've been in the workshops I do come from a church, mosque, temple or synagogue, and don't think in self-interest terms. They think that if people in positions of power or authority just knew the harm they caused, they would change. In the role-play, it becomes apparent to all that some landlords want to make as much money in the short term as they can from their buildings, no matter what the consequences for their tenants. For the most part, these landlords were indifferent to, or didn't care about, what the consequences for their tenants were—if the tenants couldn't pay, they could move. Other tenants would quickly replace them. Landlords who cared preferred stable, good tenants to short term profit maximization; other landlords had actual relationships with their tenants that were important to them. Conservatives and centrists who cared about (as distinct from those for whom facts couldn't budge ideology) these tenants had to look at the self-interest explanation. Their minds were opened to thinking differently about why the world is the way it is and what has to be done to change it in order to make it more just.

However, another circumstance also arises. In some cases landlords don't make repairs because they can't get home improvement loans. "Radicals" learned that you couldn't paint all landlords with the same brush. In these cases, a landlord could become an ally in a visit to a lending institution that might be red-lining (red-lining involves denying loans, insurance, public services, etc. to an area in order to "turn it over") a neighborhood. At this point, I would tell a story that demonstrated the collusion of city regulatory and service agencies, lenders, insurers, investors, developers and realtors who together wanted to "turn over" a neighborhood through red-lining. In the four-day workshop, participants see how to create alliances of renters, homeowners, small landlords, neighborhood merchants and local institutions to fight such a power-structure complex of interests that threatens to destroy a neighborhood. Beginning with relatively small issues—like single-building landlord-tenant disputes, tearing down a boarded-up house, getting a traffic control device at a dangerous intersection, transferring an unresponsive principal from a neighborhood elementary school, changing pricing and quality of product practices at a local store, getting rid of a local source of pollution, and similar issues is part of building a multi-issue people power organization that is based on the principle of a "lowest significant common denominator" agenda that is rooted in the morality and economic and social justice values of the world's great religions and the small "d" democratic tradition.

There was another side of the learning. To the extent that people didn't want to organize themselves to develop the people power to address their circumstances, then just to that extent conservatives were right: if people were unwilling to organize to bring about change when a real possibility for such organizing presented itself, then it became the fault of the people that they were in their circumstances. Indeed, there are circumstances in which people prefer being victims to taking the risk of becoming change agents. But there was now an important change in the idea "fault of the people." It was now the job of leaders and organizers to challenge people to act on their values and interests. To deny to people the possibility for action when believable proposals to act are made is to deny them the freedom to choose to become participants in a struggle for their own liberation, and to argue that only some other agent can accomplish that liberation.

Conflict Tactics

Introduction

Generally, "conflict tactics" are thought of as militant, confrontational, "direct action." While sometimes effective in winning a demand, these tactics rarely engage large numbers of everyday people (except in unusual circumstances—think of the freedom rides and sit-ins or the UC Berkeley Free Speech Movement), who may applaud those so engaged, but don't think of themselves as possibly being among them. Usually, such tactics rely on the dedication of young people.

In the theoretical discussion above, I describe how a role-play situation is used to move people to understand that there may be material or other conflicts of interest at stake in circumstances they consider to be unjust. It is not simply that decision-makers "don't know" the consequences of their acts, or even that they are incompetent in what they do. They may have political, economic, social or other interests that are more important to them. This is a liberating lesson because it allows people to recognize that, at a minimum, they must affect their adversary's interests if they are to change his/her behavior, and at a maximum they might have to create new structures with different incentives if they want to create a more just social order. It is in this change that the possibility of building something that can lead to transformational change emerges. Everyday people have to learn this lesson to take steps to alter the present concentration of wealth and power that is at the root of the issues of democratic participation, social and economic justice, and sustainable development that might be of concern to any of us. Building power that has the capacity for transformational action requires engaging large numbers of everyday people who do not think of themselves as "activists." The imaginative use of conflict tactics can change that.

The second lesson learned in the role play is about tactics. Building something with the capacity to bring about radical change requires winning victories along the way, but there is a double-vision focus here: winning concrete benefits from struggle, on the one hand, and changing the relations of power, on the other. The two are interconnected: one looks at the former as a tool to build the latter, and the latter as a tool to accomplish the former.

Meetings with Decision-Makers

Even before the meeting with a "decision-maker," there is an opportunity for teaching people about power. A group makes a request for a meeting to a decision-maker whose scope of authority includes resolving the problem of concern to the group. "Mr. Traffic Engineer, we would like to meet with you about a problem we are experiencing in our neighborhood." Or, "Madame Mayor, we would like to meet with you about the 'x', 'y', or 'z' problem facing our community." Or, "Mr. Bank Manager, we'd like to meet with you about the foreclosures and evictions that are taking place in our neighborhood." Or, "Mr. Landlord, we would like to meet with you about the recent notice we received announcing a $100.00 a month rent increase in our apartments."

The targeted person can say "yes" or "no" to the request for a meeting. What if she or he says "no?" The refusal to meet now requires a response. Perhaps 25 – 50 phone calls are made to the person's office saying, "we understand that you've refused to meet with us. If this is so, we'd like you to reconsider this refusal. We would like you to meet with our group." Most of the time that will be sufficient to turn the "no" into a "yes." If it's not, then a series of incremental, but rapidly escalating, tactics must be pursued. Those who thought a simple request for a meeting would be met with a positive response are being taught by the decision-maker that they must do more. The typical argument between militants and moderates that takes place in many organizations is avoided because the decision-maker forces the moderates to move to a more militant step or abandon their substantive goal. On the other hand, if the meeting is agreed to, the militants will have to acknowledge that, in this case, "reasonableness" worked.

In the role play, the person playing the adversary is usually able to use a number of divide and conquer tactics to prevent the meeting from achieving anything more than letting people vent their frustration or anger. (And if that's all that happens, the lesson learned by everyday people is a confirmation of their usually-held view that "you can't fight City Hall," or "you can't beat the money.")

Among the things the role-player adversary does to control the meeting are:

- invite many people to speak; the decision-maker, in effect, chairs the meeting—if anyone starts to pin him/her down, another person is recognized;

- if someone gets insulting or too-militant, threaten to leave the meeting (or in fact walk out), leaving the group hopelessly divided between its militant and moderate members;
- offer a proposal that gives the responsibility for the problem to the people experiencing it, so that the burden of "repair" is on them. (I've many times offered a tenant group that I would pay for the materials if they would organize themselves to do the needed repairs in the building—and sometimes had groups take me up on it!)
- etc, etc, etc.

After dividing and confusing the group with my responses to what they have to say, they agree that they need a spokesperson (or spokespersons team); a step-by-step process for presenting their case—including telling stories in the beginning that allow those present to eliminate from their minds the "don't know" theory of why an adversary doesn't respond; caucusing (a "time-out") to talk among themselves if they get confused or divided; a cut-off point when they end the negotiations if they aren't resolving anything, and; a next step if either agreement is reached or if action is required.

The most difficult thing for most groups to do is end a session. They want to keep talking. They do not recognize that "dialog" is not what this session should be about. Dialog favors the status quo: we can talk about the problem forever. If we think the problem isn't being solved because the system's representative doesn't know about it, or is incompetent to deal with it, then our informed discussion and concrete ideas of how to move forward might be appropriate. But if there are different interests at stake, and no agreement is being reached, then we must do something that will adversely affect the interests of the decision-maker on the other side of the table.

It is often, indeed typically, the case that an adversary will not say "no" to our proposal(s). There are corporate seminars in "fogging" that are designed to train public relations personnel how to obscure questions rather than make them clear. I call the vagueness that is often heard "mush." You can't fight mush. There's no resistance. We need clarity because without clarity we will be unable to make the moral case to our own members and constituency, let alone to potential allies and the media, that further action is required. Our side's spokesperson must say, "Mr/Ms _____, we are going to take what you are now telling us as a 'no.' The spokesperson then turns to the group and says something like, "All of you who agree with me raise your hand." If there isn't an overwhelming lifting of the hands, a caucus is required. If there is, the spokesperson now turns to the "target," as s/he is sometimes called, and says, "Thank you for your time. The meeting is now closed."

You would be surprised at how many times agreements are reached after this point. The adversary now recognizes that this group isn't going to be left in disarray, and that something will follow upon the "no." S/he decides a "yes" is less costly than a fight. A "yes" can be agreement, a mutually agreed upon compromise, or a new proposal that solves the problem.

One of the things I teach in the role-play is what I call "planned stupidity." Because the people you meet with on the other side go to "fogging" training sessions, they learn to make the situation unclear because lack of clarity is their ally. So is "dialogue." We are not interested in a dialog. We are interested in responses to specific proposals we place before an appropriate decision-maker who has authority to respond to our proposals. I can't tell you how often I have been in a negotiation in which the party on the other side of the table goes into a long discussion that, when you boil it down, is beating around the bush. S/he is then invariably taken aback when our side's spokesperson says something like, "Thank you. Now could you tell us your response to our proposal #1; we'd like a 'yes' or a 'no'."

As a matter of fact, the higher the degree of formal education held by our side's spokesperson(s), the more difficult it is for them to learn to act in this way. They think the meeting a debating match. They want to score points and show how smart they are. No matter how smart or articulate they are, they become unwitting participants in the other side's "fogging" agenda. For one reason, when the spokesperson starts showing how smart he is, there is the introduction of a more elaborate argument, and there are people on our side of the table who may have different views. As a matter of fact, once a spokesperson gets hooked in this way, there is a strong likelihood that the discipline of others not speaking will break down because some other member of our group who thinks he is smart now wants to introduce a "clincher" argument. Etc., etc. Often I've had to pass a note to a spokesperson that says "caucus"—so that we can take a time-out and get back on our agenda, not the opposition's.)

Whether the result of the meeting is a "no" (a disagreement) or a "yes," there are after-the-meeting organization building activities that should take place. There is *reflection*—connecting deeply held values to the specific situation) on the meaning of what was done here today. This reflection might draw upon religious or secular democratic materials. A skillful reflection adds deep meaning to the action that just took place. There is *celebration*—recognizing the history makers we are creating in our organization by giving credit to spokespersons, floor monitors, turnout work done by leaders and otherwise acknowledging roles played by people in the organization. Our work is creating a new story of "our people" making history. An *interpretation*, typically provided by one of the leaders of the group, provides a common message that participants will take home and share with others who ask the skeptic's question, "What did you waste your time on at that meeting?" or the interested person's less-cynical inquiry. A brief *evaluation* asks people how they felt about the experience (*subjective evaluation*), and compares pre-set objectives with actual experience and results (*objective evaluation*) so that learning takes place for all who participated. A more elaborate leadership evaluation will come later—as soon after the experience as possible so that its memory is accurate. *Socializing*—a party, coffee, whatever—might also be announced so that participants can better get to know one another. And a *next step*, already agreed upon—including options based on the decision-maker's response—will ask people to come to 'x' where whatever is next in the campaign or the organization's work will take place. In the case of a "no," the next step is likely to be an action in what will be a campaign to turn the "no" into a "yes." If the fight undertaken is one within the capability of the group, then the battle will be won. If not, defeat may follow. (The discussion of winnable campaigns, the varying time frames for winnability—depending on the experience and size of the group it could be from six weeks to two years, and the importance of initial victories to overcome past experiences of defeat is beyond the purview of this essay. A discussion of "winnability" can be found in my book, *A Community Organizer's Tale: People and Power in San Francisco.*)

Further, a more formal *educational* discussion, seminar or workshop might, if the issue at hand was redlining or foreclosures, explore credit unions, publicly owned banks, anti-trust legislation, tighter regulation and other policy options in relation to financial institutions. It might involve exploring the history of the Populists, and their efforts to deal with banks. Here, curiosity—the motivation to learn—is aroused by the experience of a conflict with power. In this case, it is a bank manager—i.e. the system—that is doing the initial "education" of the people. Of course leadership and organizers are engaged in interpretative discussions with campaign participants—but the initial "curriculum" is provided by the behavior and utterances of the manager.

Key Principles

The campaigns that begin with these face-to-face meetings implement three tactical principles that began with the request for a meeting. These are not original to me. The ideas of personalizing the opposition, polarizing the situation, and "the action is in the reaction" were introduced by Saul Alinsky. This is an elaboration of them.

1. Personalize the opposition: Using the example of a bank manager, who we'll call "Mr. Jones", the issues about which the group wants to meet are foreclosures and evictions from foreclosed houses. The delegation wants to propose to him that he (a) place a moratorium on the foreclosure of the "x," "y," and "z," families who are part of the delegation or represented by the group, and re-negotiate their loans, and that he withdraw eviction notices to families "a," "b," and "c". (*Note: not "demand" or "request", but "propose". Not "request" because it means that you're only asking. Not "demand" because some of your people will prefer being polite, and you will divide your group at the outset over the use of the word. I have yet to find anyone who objects to "propose."*)

Central to doing this correctly is the extended role-play before hand in which, in this case, someone plays the bank manager. One of the things the role player says is, "I don't have the authority to do that." The "people's side" responds, "Then we want an appointment with you within 30 days at which time either you have obtained the authority or you bring to the meeting a person who has the authority to act on our proposals." (In fact, the manager probably won't have the authority, but someone does—and if the heat on that branch is high enough the manager will be able to produce that someone.) You set the appointment then. (There's lots more in the role-play; another key phrase to be learned is that "We are sure you can find someone in your bank to come to the meeting with authority to speak for the bank on this matter.")

Why is this important? First, an analogy: people think awful things about Congress—but not their Congressperson. Similarly, people think awful things about Bank of America, Wells Fargo, Chase, Citibank, etc, but don't think so badly about their branch where the tellers are nice to them, the manager may have waived a bounced check fee, and the bank donates to local nonprofits. The bank manager has to be given the opportunity to do the right thing, even though we may think the odds are 99:1 that he won't or can't.

2. Polarize the situation. The bank manager's refusal to do the right thing—agree to get the "right person" to a next meeting—is the source of energy for a campaign to make the bank do the right thing. That refusal makes moderates into militants. People who would not have handed out flyers in front of the bank and engaged in conversations with account holders as they entered are now willing to do that and more. (Indeed, as an or-

ganizer, I've often had to persuade initially too-moderate people not to now become too militant.) The conversations and flyers might ask account holders to close their accounts. The campaign's specific, well-researched proposal(s) (simple, not complex, but rooted in law and/or bank regulations and practices) eliminate the theory "the system is incompetent." You have given the system a way to competently act to solve the problem; it has refused to accept it. That leaves the theoretical understanding you want people to reach—that at least in some instances the system has different interests than those of your group and, perhaps, of the millions of families who are being foreclosed across the country. They want to make a buck. You want people to have decent, safe, affordable, sanitary housing in communities of their choice.

3. The action is in the reaction. In the role-play, what must be accomplished is an agreement that the spokesperson team will only accept either a "yes" or "no" answer. As a matter of fact, as an organizer I generally prefer a "no" to a "yes" in first encounters with decision-makers. But note this caveat: that's because I'm pretty confident that our group can turn the "no" into a "yes." I want people to learn how to fight for justice. If agreement comes too easily, they won't learn much about the use of nonviolent conflict tactics to accomplish their goals.

Conclusion

We are now in a period of great opportunity…and great danger. Activists have to be careful not to generalize to the population as a whole from their own anger and analysis. There already are people whose general view is that the banks are just in business to make money, and that all their rhetoric, use of community rooms for public meetings, donations to the local school, jars of goodies for dogs, balloons for kids, etc are window dressing to accomplish that result. But it may be that there is still a gulf between those so convinced and the majority, or a significant minority, who remain to be convinced. This group must become engaged if we are to accomplish the broader program of claiming and winning democracy, social and economic justice and a sustainable environment.

The opportunity is building a truly transformational movement. The danger is that our action will unleash a repressive reaction, or that defeat will lead to a return to feelings of hopelessness, powerlessness and despair, accompanied by continued and expanding social and economic problems, and even greater concentration of wealth and power in the hands of the few.

Another danger is an illusion that is unfortunately being propagated by people who should know better—that there is already a "mass movement". We are far from that. There is motion. That is good. There is a whole shift in the country's debate that is expressed in the anger at the "1%." That is good too. There is still a need to move many, many, many more people into some form of action—action that will make use of the personalize, polarize, and "the action is in the reaction" tactical principles.

Here's something to think about that will give you a sense of scale: in 2011 there were demonstrations in Israel for greater economic and social justice in domestic policies. For us in the United States to reach a population-equivalent scale to their turnout, we would have to have 18 million people demonstrating in Washington, DC. We aren't there yet. If we build properly, we can get there.

*About the Author

Mike Miller spent most of his life in the San Francisco Bay Area. He was born in San Francisco's Mission District, and raised in Sunnydale Housing Project, attended UC Berkeley where he was a leader in the early student movement organization called SLATE (1957/58, 1960/62), and did graduate work in sociology at Columbia University and Berkeley. His first organizing job was with public housing tenants on New York's Lower Eastside (1959).

From 1962 through 1966 he was a full-time field secretary for the Student Nonviolent Coordinating Committee (SNCC). He then directed a community organizing project for Saul Alinsky in Kansas City, MO, two community organizing efforts in San Francisco (Mission Coalition Organization and All Peoples Coalition), a city-wide campaign for a slate who beat a conservative slate and won a majority of school board seats, and the statewide Citizens Action League that won lifeline utility rates in California. In 1972, he started ORGANIZE! Training from which he continues his organizing work. From 2001-2004 he edited the quarterly, *Social Policy*. His organizing work history includes directing local and statewide projects, building sponsor committees, leading labor and community organizing workshops, consulting, mentoring and lecturing in the field.

He taught community organizing, urban studies or political science at the University of California, Stanford, Notre Dame, San Francisco State, Hayward State and Lone Mountain College.

His articles have appeared in Christianity and Crisis; Commission On Religion & Race Reports; Social Policy; New Conversations; Organizing; The Organizer; The Ark; Citizen Participation; Berkeley Journal Of Sociology; The Boston Review; the liberal democrat; The Movement; Dissent; Studies On The Left; Working U.S.A.; Generations; Race, Poverty and the Environment; Poverty & Race Research and Action Report; International Journal of Urban Planning and Research; and other periodicals, and in the newspapers Sun Reporter and San Francisco Examiner. His book, A Community Organizer's Tale: People and Power in San Francisco, was published by Heyday in 2009. He has authored chapters on issues related to community organizing, democracy and social movements in books edited by Harry Boyte, Wilson Carey McWilliams and Massimo Teodori.

He lives in San Francisco's Noe Valley neighborhood with his dog Chloe, and has three grown stepchildren, and a grandchild from each of them.

CPSIA information can be obtained at www.ICGtesting.com
Printed in the USA
LVOW05s0827200814

399844LV00010B/168/P